D0090074

[BRAIN CANDY]

[SCIENCE, PARADOXES, PUZZLES, LOGIC, AND ILLOGIC TO NOURISH YOUR NEURONS **]**

THREE RIVERS PRESS
NEW YORK

BRAIN CANDY

[**GARTH SUNDEM**]

Copyright © 2010 by Garth Sundem

All rights reserved.
Published in the United States by Three Rivers Press,
an imprint of the Crown Publishing Group,
a division of Random House, Inc., New York.
www.crownpublishing.com

Three Rivers Press and the Tugboat design are registered
trademarks of Random House, Inc.

Library of Congress Cataloging-in-Publication Data

Sundem, Garth.
Brain candy / Garth Sundem.—1st ed.
p. cm.
1. Puzzles. 2. Amusements. I. Title.
GV1493.S869 2010
793.73—dc22   2009050930

978-0-307-58803-6

Printed in the United States of America

Design by Maria Elias

1 3 5 7 9 10 8 6 4 2

First Edition

To Lief, my little boy with a very big brain

CONTENTS

INTRODUCTION

Remember the FDA food pyramid and your horror
when you learned that it takes six loaves of sprouted wheat bread to
balance the effects of a thimbleful of sour apple Nerds? The same is
supposed to be true of your brain: to avoid vegetative zombiism, you
need a semester's worth of particle physics to counteract that *Dancing
with the Stars* marathon you watched on Saturday. Make it two semes-
ters if you scan the checkout-stand headlines.

Right?

Wrong.

This book has punk'd the pyramid.

In these pages, you can trick your brain into thinking it's watching that
reality-television marathon when in fact it's exploring cutting-edge topics in neuroscience, psychology, behavioral economics, neuroanatomy,
game theory, cognitive science, and more.

In short, what's here is candy. But it's candy that's *good for your
brain.*

Did you know that country music leads to a higher suicide rate
among whites? Have you seen the neural signature of a daydream?
Did you know that the smell of shoe leather can arrest epileptic seizure? That mirror neurons create human morality, or that liars are
biologically different from truth-tellers? That red beats blue in Olympic grappling contests? If any of these topics intrigue you—or if you,
like me, love geeking out on puzzles and illogic and perception oddi-
ties and questionable morality, and want to understand a bit more
how the spittings of what is essentially a three-pound electric sausage
make us human—read on.

. . .

Ten years ago, this book couldn't have been written. As recently as the mid-twentieth century, neurosurgeons lobotomized patients by punching ice picks through their eye sockets and waggling them back and forth. And psychologists were amazed when a dog drooled to the soundtrack of the Westminster Bell Choir. Now neurosurgeons get an assist from fMRI-guided robots and chat with patients during tumor surgery. And psychologists have moved past drooling dogs to explore the basis of what it means to be human: consciousness, cognition, reality, free will, and the very subjective ways we experience the world.

Brain science is exploding.

And if brain science is exploding, then the niche of neuroplasticity—which describes how and how profoundly our actions shape our brains—is a nuclear bomb. You can grow your brain by flexing it in the right way, just as surely as Gold's Gym grows muscles. Your thoughts, feelings, words, and deeds are more than ephemeral whims that happen and pass—they're encoded into the basic architecture of our brains as neurons grow, die, and rewire, and as regions with different functions optimize or decay.

So flex your brain. Seriously. To put it bluntly, reading this book will make you smarter—that is, if you use it to force your brain into new, challenging terrain (see the topics "The Key to Brain Training" and "Do Crosswords Keep the Brain Young?"). A little challenge to nourish your neurons can delay the effects of Alzheimer's, and who doesn't need a little extra cerebral pop at home and in the office?

And nothing grows gray matter like disagreement. (The *New York Times* reports that the best way for adults to stimulate their brains is by "challenging the very assumptions they have worked so hard to accumulate.") Fortunately, because the majority of these topics are ripped from the headlines of leading academic journals, much is on the edge of "proven" and you will almost certainly find topics that you disagree with. Please: think, evaluate, decide, and *then* write me nasty e-mails—but before you take to the blogosphere like a winged monkey, check the original studies, referenced under topic headings at the back of the book. Also check the back of the book for scoring guidelines for the included self-tests, answers to the genius tester puzzles, and discussions of the game-theory dilemmas.

Now, sit back, get comfy (get a pencil!), and let this book turn a mirror to your mind.

[BRAIN CANDY]

COUNTRY MUSIC KILLS

Does country music make you want to grab a lariat and hang yourself from the nearest old elm tree? If so, you're not alone. Social psychologists Steven Stack and Jim Gundlach found that the more a city's radio stations play country music, the higher the white suicide rate.

Seriously.

Theirs was a big study, encompassing forty-nine metropolitan areas, and was careful to control for factors like Southernness, poverty, divorce, and gun availability. In other words, all else equal, country music kills. This was especially true when country music represented a city's sub- rather than its mainstream culture.

COOL NEUROSURGERY PAST AND PRESENT: TREPANATION THROUGH TIME

Today, trepanation, or drilling a hole in the head, is commonly used to release the pressure of swelling inside the skull. Throughout history, it's been used to treat epilepsy, migraines, mood disorders, and pretty much any other head condition that seemed to surgeons of the time as if it could be improved by seeing the light of day.

Prehistoric

This skull of a young girl dates to around 3500 B.C. The hole in the head is intentional, and postoperative bone growth shows that the patient survived the operation. Even earlier evidence for trepanation exists: Of 120 skulls at a burial site in France dated to 6500 B.C., 40 showed trepanation holes and most showed the continuing bone growth that implies survival.

Incan

While it's sometimes difficult to tell Incan trepanation from the practice of ritual, postmortem skull mutilation (charming, eh?), we nonetheless have enough evidence to tell that the practice was widespread. It's interesting to note that while the Inca were chippers (as seen here), the Maya were grinders, preferring to wear away the skull with rough rocks until exposing the brain.

Netherlands: 1494

This shows a detail from a 1494 painting by the Dutch master Hieronymus Bosch, titled *De keisnijding*, which translates to "Removing the rocks in his head."

Netherlands: 1525

This 1525 engraving from a manual titled *Handywarke of Surgeri* shows a rather Inquisition-like trepanation machine. Interestingly, the Dutch are still leading the charge for trepanning today, in the person of Dr. Bart Hughes, who claims that it promotes blood-brain volume and can return people to the enlightened, childlike state of an infant whose skull bones have not yet fused. Those wacky lowlanders!

Renaissance France

It should be noted that the physician performing this trepanation is wearing an expression similar to that of Tim Roth playing the villain Archibald Cunningham in the movie *Rob Roy*.

Enlightenment Age

Like a build-your-own-model-airplane plan, this late 1800s diagram of trepanning includes a materials list and illustrated, step-by-step directions.

SELF-TREPANATION

In the autobiographical book *Bore Hole,* Joey Mellen describes his attempts at self-trepanation. Attempts numbers one and two are unsuccessful, resulting in hospital visits and psychiatric evaluations, but no hole. He writes the following of his third attempt: "After some time there was an ominous sounding schlurp and the sound of bubbling. I drew the trepan out and the gurgling continued. It sounded like air bubbles running under the skull as they were pressed out. I looked at the trepan and there was a bit of bone in it. At last!"

Later, Mellen filmed the self-trepanation of his girlfriend, Amanda Feilding, for a film they called *Heartbeat in the Brain.*

Note: While it certainly sounds fun, most doctors recommend against self-trepanation.

INTRO TO GAME THEORY: PRISONER'S DILEMMA

Game theory was developed by big-brained people attempting world domination. For their efforts, they earned Nobel Prizes and a screaming throng of teenage fans à la mid-1960s Beatles. (OK, maybe just the first, but it's worth picturing hysterical fans throwing underwear while chanting *Nash! Nash! Nash!*)

Basically, game theory attempts to explain how people act in competitive or collaborative situations. And, more usefully in pursuit of said world domina-

Be Nice, but Not Too Nice: Game Theory Says So

In real-world relationships, rarely is there only one chance for trust or betrayal. So what's our best strategy over the long run? To answer this question, the game theorist Robert Axelrod held a Prisoner's Dilemma tournament. Each pair of players played two hundred rounds of the dilemma, trying to accumulate low jail sentences over these rounds.

The best strategy was called Tit for Tat. In it, the player cooperates the first round and then mimics the other player every move thereafter. In Axelrod's tournaments this strategy eventually created predictability and cooperation, allowing both players to consistently earn a string of six-month sentences for keeping their mouths shut.

From the tournament, Axelrod drew the following rules, which provide good commonsensical advice for many interactions, inside and out of games:

- Be Nice: cooperation benefits all

- Be Provocable: provide correction for others' meanness

- Keep It Simple: predictability breeds trust

Watching one season of the show *Survivor* demonstrates the effectiveness of these rules.

tion, it also attempts to define your best strategy in light of your opponents' likely actions.

Take, for example, this oldie but goody drawn from the hallowed halls of game theory (1950, Merrill Flood and Albert W. Tucker):

Two suspects are arrested. The police have insufficient evidence for a conviction, and, having separated the prisoners, visit each of them to offer the same deal. If one testifies for the prosecution against the other and the other remains silent, the betrayer goes free and the silent accomplice receives the full ten-year sentence. If both remain silent, both prisoners are sentenced to only six months in jail for a minor charge. If each betrays the other, each receives a five-year sentence. Each prisoner must choose to betray the other or to remain silent. Each one is assured that the other would not know about the betrayal before the end of the investigation. How should the prisoners act?

Check the back of this book for the answer—it's as good as the puzzle itself.

SOCIAL CONTAGION: HAPPINESS AND OBESITY ARE CATCHING

Social scientists Nicholas Christakis and James Fowler followed about two-thirds of the residents of Framingham, Massachusetts, as they got happy, sad, fit, and obese, and started or quit smoking. And they asked these couple-thousand residents about their friends: who did they hang out with? Now imagine a diagram showing a huge net of people who know people. Within this net, the scientists found ' clusters of obesity, happiness, and smoking. In other words, if your friends are happy, you're happy, and if your friends are obese, you're likely to be too.

That's pretty intuitive: like attracts like.

But what's interesting is that Christakis and Fowler watched these patterns *change:* if your slender friend puts on a couple pounds, you're likely to put on a couple pounds too. And so happiness, obesity, and smoking pass through a population like a contagious virus.

What's your risk of infection? Well, the data from Framingham show that if a friend becomes

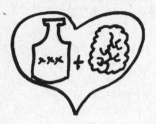

Booze Protects the Brain

Have you heard the descriptor "pickled"? It may be more than slang. An Australian study of more than ten thousand people found that moderate drinkers are about 26 percent less likely than abstainers to develop dementia in later life. The difference may be due to biology (alcohol's anti-inflammatory properties) or psychology: moderate drinkers are social.

obese, you're 57 percent more likely to become obese too. And you're at risk even if a friend of a friend gains weight—in fact, you're exactly 20 percent more likely to gain weight too (but only when measured against friends of the same gender). The good doctors measured alcohol consumption too, and found that a man changing his drinking habits has little effect on his friends, but that when a *woman* starts to drink more, both her male and female friends will drink more, themselves.

So why gamble on your friends' behaviors? Why not hole up in a cabin in Montana where your happiness is self-sufficient? It turns out that happiness is more catching than sadness. Specifically, a happy friend boosts your mood by 9 percent, while an unhappy friend lowers it by 7 percent. As long as you're not specifically picking unhappy friends, the happiness gamble of extending your social network as widely as possible should pay off.

You can read much more about social contagion in the duo's very cool book, *Connected: The Surprising Power of Our Social Networks and How They Shape Our Lives.*

TOO DUMB TO KNOW IT

To be blunt, it's possible to be so dumb that you're unaware of your own idiocy (look to the left, look to the right . . . you get the point; that is, unless you're dumb). Put another way, many dumb people think they're smart. This, of course, is dumb.

How dumb are they? (Insert punch line here.)

In the classic study of overconfident idiots, Justin Kruger and David Dunning of Cornell University found that subjects scoring in the lowest quartile on tests of humor, grammar, and logic were also the most faulty in their self-assessments, predicting they would score in the 62nd percentile, when in fact they scored in the 12th.

Photocopy. Cut. And post this near your office watercooler.

The Lemon-Juice Thief

In their article in the *Journal of Personality and Social Psychology*, Dunning and Kruger offer the following case to illustrate overconfidence due to idiocy:

In 1995, a man named McArthur Wheeler was arrested for robbing two banks. The police had no trouble tracking him down: During the robberies he'd made no visible attempt at disguise and so had been captured clearly by the banks' security cameras. When the cops showed him the damning surveillance footage, Wheeler protested, "But I wore the juice!" Apparently, he believed that rubbing his face with lemon juice would render it invisible to video cameras.

SMARTER EVERY DAY

IQ is supposedly an objective measure of innate intelligence. It's how smart you are.

Period.

But then why is humanity's IQ increasing? Are our brains getting better? Our blossoming genius is so profound that every twenty years or so we need a new, harder IQ test just to keep up. (The average person from the year 1900 would score near 70 on today's test, or on the edge of profound mental retardation.)

I've got the brain of a four-year-old. I'll bet he was glad to be rid of it.

—Groucho Marx

People have suggested that this phenomenon is created by better diets, improved schooling, smaller families, or more liberal child-rearing techniques.

But is there something else going on here?

It turns out that only specific parts of the IQ test show significant increases: modern humans are better than our forebears at spotting abstract patterns and at reordering scrambled pictures, but we are no better than Jefferson, Washington, and Abigail Adams at memorizing sequences of numbers, and our scores for vocabulary and general knowledge are similar.

It turns out the question of increasing IQ is one of priorities and not one of intelligence. While modern humans place value on spotting abstract patterns and connecting widely disparate ideas, our ancestors thought abstract reasoning was silly, preferring a "show me the corn" focus on concrete reasoning.

And so researchers watch with interest today's shifting priorities. Specifically, we increasingly devalue the ability to store information. No longer does schooling focus on memorizing dates and places and the Declaration of Independence. To a large degree, we've off-loaded the storage function of our brains to Google. If we can so easily get information, why memorize it? (This is like a couple generations ago when we realized that machines could add, subtract, multiply, and divide . . . and lost the ability to do so ourselves.)

Are we living at the top of an IQ bubble in which we can both reason abstractly and recall concrete information? Eventually, will the devaluation of memorization lead to underperformance on the concrete knowledge sections of the IQ test, dragging our overall IQ scores down? Will our IQ bubble pop like the tech and housing bubbles?

In short, are we due to get dumber?

IQ Cycle

As described above, every twenty years or so we design a new, harder test to compensate for steadily rising scores. One effect of this cycle is that around year nineteen of each test's life span, fewer people earn low scores and fewer public-school students qualify for low-IQ support programs. The enrollment in these programs shrinks and so does their funding. Then, with the adoption of a new, harder test, a glut of students qualifies, overrunning the support system.

THE KEY TO BRAIN TRAINING

You know those books: the ones that promise to keep your brain young through a training regimen of puzzles and thought exercises (wait a minute . . .). Well, it turns out there's one easy key

Eye Hack: Ehrenstein Illusion

Look at the curved lines that create the diamond's sides. They're straight. Really.

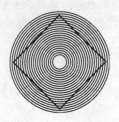

to brain training: challenging new experiences.

Once you've done your nth Sudoku, your brain's as wired for it as it'll ever be. Doing more Sudoku only reinforces these existing pathways. If your goal is to remain good at Sudoku in your later years, great; if you'd like more far-reaching cognitive ben-

efits, it's time to move on. The same is true of timed math problems, memory games, or even crosswords.

Instead, to enjoy the effects of brain training you need to present the brain with tasks that force it to create new connections between cells. If you understand immediately how you'll go about completing a puzzle, it's probably familiar enough that it's not worth doing.

GAME THEORY MAKE BRAIN BIG: COLONEL BLOTTO I

Colonel Blotto has six soldiers in his command. The opposing colonel has six as well. There are three simultaneous battles. In each battle, the colonel who sends the most troops wins. The colonel who wins the most battles wins the war. To keep things (somewhat) simple, the colonels can only choose between sending combinations of 1,1,4, or 1,2,3, or 2,2,2 troops into the battles.

What's Blotto's best strategy? (Stumped? Check the answer key at the back of the book.)

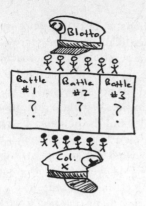

THE GUILTY PLEASURE OF SCHADENFREUDE

If you're thirsty and you drink, your brain feels pleasure. You feel this same pleasure, borne of satisfying a physical need, when someone you envy is brought low.

We call this feeling schadenfreude, but researchers at the National Institute of Radiological Sciences in Japan call it dopamine release in the ventral striatum. The thirstier or more envious we are, the more dopamine released when the need is met. Only after our cerebral cortex steps in to evaluate the reason for our pleasure does the neurological experience of schadenfreude diverge from that of quenching thirst: water stays pure, while schadenfreude brings a layer of guilt.

This shared pathway of physi-

Zen Mind

A man traveling across a field encountered a tiger. He fled, the tiger coming after him. Coming to a precipice, he caught hold of the root of a wild vine and swung himself down over the edge. The tiger sniffed at him from above. Trembling, the man looked down to where, far below, another tiger was waiting to eat him. Only the vine sustained him.

Two mice, one white and one black, little by little started to gnaw away the vine. The man saw a luscious strawberry near him. Grasping the vine with one hand, he plucked the strawberry with the other.

How sweet it tasted!

cal and emotional need suggests that complex emotions like schadenfreude are no less deeply ingrained in our neural systems than basic desires for things like food and water.

GAME THEORY MAKE BRAIN BIG: COLONEL BLOTTO II

This time Colonel Blotto has twelve soldiers to split across three battlefields. The opposing colonel has the same. Again, the number of troops they use for each battle must stay even or increase (1,3,8 is allowed while 8,3,1 and 1,8,3 are not).

What's Blotto's best strategy? (Stumped? Check the answer key at the back of the book.)

MIRROR NEURONS: YOUR ACTIONS IN MY HEAD

It's easy to imagine the benefit of being able to predict others' intentions: is Thog throwing spear at mastodon, or is Thog throwing spear at me? Is wife approaching with large holiday fruitcake as food gift or as weapon?

To answer these questions, we try out the actions we see in our own brains and then interpret what our intentions would be if we were doing the same thing. (Brain to self: *If I were wearing that sadistically gleeful expression while approaching with holiday fruitcake, the aproachee would be wise to flee . . .*)

Makes sense, right? The interesting thing is, it turns out we have special cells that do only this. They're called mirror neurons.

Most think that mirror neurons are also the basis of empathy. In his very good book, *Mirroring People*, UCLA researcher Marco Iacoboni points out that when we watch movie stars kissing on the big screen, mirror neurons create in our brains the partial sensation that we're the ones doing the smooching; when we see someone in pain, mirror neurons make us feel a muted version of this pain too.

And the power of mirror neurons extends beyond interpreting large-scale, physical actions. Iacoboni showed this with his now-famous teacup experiment, in which subjects watched three videotaped scenes of a hand lifting a teacup: one in which there was no context (only a disembodied hand holding a cup with no background), one that the brain quickly interpreted as showing someone in the act of cleaning up, and one that the brain saw as lifting the cup to drink. Mirror neurons didn't have much to say about the simple holding scene. They didn't much care for the cleaning scene, either. But gol-darn if they didn't like the drinking! They fired just as they would in a person about to actually drink tea.

In emotionally flat scenes, no mirror neurons; but in the scene of anticipation, mirror neurons go boom, providing in viewers a partial version of the tea drinker's visceral experience.

We feel what others feel.

Mirror neurons may also be responsible for our desire to imitate people. When a person you're speaking with leans in, smiles, and brushes back her hair, you do the same. In a more scientific study of this "social mirroring," subjects who were shown frowning faces frowned, and subjects who were shown smiling faces smiled.

Researchers blame this on mirror neurons: We feel another person's actions inside our head and so are able to mimic them. And the more we mimic, the more our conversation partner experiences our empathy and the more we bond. And so mirror neurons create social connection.

And check this out: when we can't mimic, we can't understand. Researcher Paula Niedenthal forced viewers of smiling and frowning faces to hold a pencil between their teeth, removing their ability to mimic by moving their own mouths. Thus restricted, they were much worse at determining who was frowning and who was smiling.

Either way, mirror neurons allow us to know what others are thinking, feeling, and planning. They're empathy sticks and by forcing us to feel the effects of our behavior, may also form the basis of morality.

Whether they can create world peace and bring every little girl a pony is yet to be seen.

Self-Test: The Robin Hood Morality Quiz

Read the following story and then rank Robin, Maid Marian, the sheriff of Nottingham, and Little John from most to least moral (then check the back of the book for interpretation):

The sheriff of Nottingham has finally caught Robin Hood and Little John! Instead of killing them immediately, he makes the mistake of all storybook villains in simply stashing them in the dungeon. Despite their track record of heroics, there the two benevolent outlaws rot—until Maid Marian shows up pleading her love for Robin and begging for his release. Sure, says the sheriff, if Marian will sleep with him.

She does. Robin and Little John are released. But when Maid Marian tells Robin the truth of how she earned their freedom, Robin dumps her faster than a leprous leech. Little John defends her behavior and offers his lifelong devotion if she will ride away from Sherwood with him forever.

She does. The end.

WILD KINGDOM: SENTIENT ELEPHANTS

When you drop a mirror into a fish bowl or parakeet cage, house pets attack. They mistake the reflected image of themselves for an intruder and decide it must die (or at least be massively intimidated by puffed feathers or flexed gills). Humans, in the presence of a mirror, recognize our own reflections and quickly begin to groom. This is self-awareness.

What about elephants?

Researchers at the Bronx Zoo decided to find out. They smudged elephants with paint and held mirrors in front of the soiled elephants. Sure enough, the elephants recognized themselves and began exploring the smudge marks with their trunks.

So far, the only other non-humans that pass the mirror self-recognition test are apes and dolphins. Researchers attribute ape, dolphin, elephant, and human self-awareness to our similarly complex social structures.

Zen Mind

One day Chuang Tzu and a friend were walking along a riverbank. Chuang Tzu smiled and said, "How delightfully the fishes are enjoying themselves in the water!"

"You are not a fish," his friend said. "How do you know whether the fishes are enjoying themselves?"

"You are not me," Chuang Tzu said. "How do you know that I do not know that the fishes are enjoying themselves?"

NEURAL NETS KNOW ALL

Imagine you wanted to predict when sheep would chew. (Don't ask why . . . just *imagine*.) Here's how you would do it: Attach speakers to the tops of sheep heads to broadcast chewing sounds. Collect chewing sounds and their times in a massive database. Feed these data into

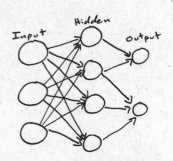

Neural Network

In a neural network certain inputs lead to certain outputs. The mechanism between the two doesn't really matter.

a neural net, which would recognize input (times) and output (chewing or not chewing) and eventually learn to predict when one leads to the other.

This is what neural nets do: They predict the future by quantifying the past.

A relatively simple example of this in the brain is the hippocampus. Electrical signals go in one end and are spit out the other. Every time a certain stimulus arrives, it goes out another certain way, like dropping a ball into a pegboard maze and watching it bounce through the matrix to a predefined exit. Only, in the hippocampus there happen to be millions and millions of inputs and outputs.

How does this electricity know how to route itself inside the hippocampus? The neural net learns how.

When you're young, you drop millions of test balls into your hippocampus. They bounce through the matrix and pop out at random exits. Some happen to exit at the right places and only these complete start-to-finish pathways are reinforced (see neuroplasticity). Eventually, the neural net of your hippocampus learns which paths are successful and becomes able to correctly route these inputs.

In artificial use, in addition

to the very important problem of sheep mastication, neural nets have been used in face and handwriting recognition, chess software, hybrid vehicle control, data mining, attempts at stock market modeling, and e-mail spam filtering. Neural nets have also been used to create an artificial nose. This sniffer uses a chemical sensor to recognize the many little bits that make up a smell (inputs) and a neural net to predict what source these bits come from (output). These artificial noses will soon be the new canaries: Put them in the presence of questionable odors and they will define the danger.

BRAIN CHIP: NEURAL NETS AND THE ARTIFICIAL HIPPOCAMPUS

The science of prosthetics has evolved from the wooden stump, through the metal hook, through the plastic look-alike, through a limb with robotic function, to today's limb with robotic function controlled by the brain. Commonly these prostheses replace an appendage, but we can re-

place hearts and can almost replace lungs and livers, too.

But what if it's your brain that needs replacement, due to stroke, injury, autism, Alzheimer's, cerebral palsy, or the like? Enter neurocognitive prosthetics, which are (or will be) implants that support or take the place of malfunctioning regions of the brain.

If this sounds far-fetched, consider the fact that we already do this with cochlear implants that replace the eardrum and directly stimulate the auditory nerves. And the next step—not simply stimulating the brain, but acting *as the brain*—is in the works.

The hippocampus is a fairly straightforward region of the brain. If it works, you can code new memories; if it doesn't, you can't. Basically, it accepts electrical stimuli and emits corresponding electrical results, like a complex series of ricochets. The same stimulus produces the same response every time. Despite its simplicity and despite the fact that it's one of the brain's most studied regions, exactly how it works is anyone's guess.

The innovation of researchers at the University of Southern California was in *not caring* how it works. Instead, they realized that what matters is its function: Electricity enters one place and leaves at another. If they could simply reproduce the in/out pattern, they could replicate its function without caring about the workings inside the black box. So they simply fired electricity into the maze and charted where it came out . . . millions and millions of times. They then programmed these inputs and outputs onto a computer chip.

It worked great!

That was in 2003. Recent artificial hippocampus chatter is way down since the initial wow factor, but the device continues to work its way through rats toward monkeys, and most involved with the project agree that it's only a matter of time before it hits humans.

Hatchibombotar via Flickr.com

Eye Hack: Cornsweet Illusion

Which half of this rectangle is lighter? The right half, of course! Actually, they're exactly the same shade; only, a gradient in the center goes from dark to light, implying the change in shade. To check, cover the centerline and compare the two sides.

PIECE OF MIND: HIPPOCAMPUS

When we learn something, it's the hippocampus that packages it for storage. Think of it like a vault that accepts deposits of new information but off-loads items to off-site storage.

Interestingly, the architecture of your hippocampus is changing right now as you read this sentence. That's no surprise: New neurons are born in your hippocampus every second. But only learning keeps these new neurons alive. Researchers showed this in 2007 when they stained rat neurons, trained the rats, and then counted these stained neurons. The rats that successfully learned from the training retained more of these stained neurons than rats that experienced the same training, but failed to learn.

So passive appreciation is not enough to keep your hippocampus kicking. To grow neurons, information needs to not only hit your hippocampus, but also be processed through it into learning.

ABNORMAL PSYCH: HM (PATIENT)

Henry Molaison is one of the most studied subjects in psy-

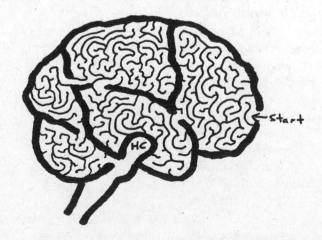

chiatric history. After surgeons removed most of his hippocampus in an attempt to control debilitating epileptic seizures, HM lost the ability to store new memories. Interestingly, largely unimpaired were his working memory (allowing him to read and socialize), short-term memory (allowing him to retain facts for short periods of time), and his long-term memory (allowing him to recall events prior to his surgery). HM continued to perform normally on IQ tests.

Speed Shrinking

You know speed dating, but what about speed therapy? At speed shrinking parties around the country, you can unload your psycho-baggage and get Twitter-esque feedback from a real, live therapist—in a three-minute session. Pioneered by humorist Susan Shapiro, speed shrinking is pushing toward legitimacy.

Without his hippocampus, though, he simply couldn't code new long-term memories.

But this doesn't mean that HM was incapable of learning: it seems that only his *explicit* learning—the traditional process of memorizing facts and processes—was wiped out and not his *implicit* learning. For example, his motor learning was completely unaffected and he retained the ability to create topographic memories, drawing a detailed map of the residence he had moved to five years after his surgery (but not the small-scale spatial memory of where stuff was around this residence). After many repetitions, HM also gained implicit memory of puzzle solutions: he had no conscious memory of ever seeing a puzzle before and had no flash of recognition as to its solution, but after working a puzzle many times, he could complete it more quickly than he had when attempting it the first time.

Researchers call HM's puzzle-learning *repetition priming* and suggest that it's something of a cognitive equivalent of motor learning: Over time and with enough repetitions, learning seeps into the structures of our brains without the fast-track bundling of the hippocampus.

LOGIC OF ILLOGIC: THE TRICKY SECONDARY MARKET AND WHY ECONOMISTS HATE PSYCHOLOGY

Blue Devil basketball tickets are a hot commodity: There are far more fans than seats. And so some students enter a ticket lottery.

After one of these lotteries, Duke researchers posing as ticket scalpers found that students who lost the raffle were willing to pay $170 for a seat, while students who won tickets would only sell their seats for an average of $2,400.

This shucks common economic theory: the same seat for the same game should have a set price. Why would students on either side of the admittance fence place widely differing values on the same good?

Blame it on psychology, specifically the endowment effect (what we have is worth more than what we don't). Also, to accept their inability to attend the game, students who lost the raffle had to devalue the importance of attendance: they convince themselves, "It's OK, I didn't *really* want to go, anyway."

While winning students' astronomical price tag was a form of gloating: "Ha, ha, look what I've got and look how much it's worth!"

This is why economists hate psychology (not so with behavioral economists, but that's another story). And it's this disconnect between economics and psychology that makes for a sticky secondary market: When psychology swings against demand, items sit on shelves. And when psychology hypes demand, scalpers, speculators, and eBay resellers prosper.

The secondary market's even more exciting when an item's intentionally underpriced. This is what happens when you start an eBay auction at $1.00. And it's what Bruce Springsteen inadvertently did during his 2009 tour when he set prices for his New Jersey Meadowlands tickets at $95, thereby chucking StubHub and other scalping sites a bone of gargantuan proportions.

Eye Hack: The Hermann Grid

Focus on one black dot. Of course, this is impossible—all the dots are white—but because our mind gives undue weight to the edges of things, we see these black-bounded dots as black.

Your brain is used to trying to win rock, paper, scissors. And so if you happen to see rock coming down, it's much easier to adjust your throw mid-flight to shoot paper than it is to adjust your throw to scissors (both, by the way, are cheating). In other words, deliberately playing to lose hurts your brain. Researchers measured this by showing subjects a string of RPS symbols on a computer screen, with a symbol every 1.5 seconds. The researchers had one group respond to the images by shooting winning symbols and another group respond by intentionally shooting losing symbols. To lose, subjects' prefrontal cortexes had to squirt some serious oxyhemoglobin to override the natural impulse to win, and reaction times were slower. This is executive function overriding impulse.

Speaking of games and executive function, it is specifically this prefrontal ability to override impulse that is lacking in pathological gamblers, as well as in populations with alcohol dependence and Tourette's syndrome.

ROSHAMBO WINNERS GUIDE

Humans are very, very bad at being random. In roshambo— aka rock, paper, scissors—this leads to probabilities and patterns that you can exploit to give your RPS opponent(s) severe and repeated thumpings. There are two ways to go about this: knowing the psychology and creating new psychology.

First, it's useful to understand the generally held associations of the three symbols: Rock is solid, aggressive, and steadfast; scissors are aggressive in a more tactical way; and paper is flaccid, like shooting a very wet toilet paper spitball. Because of these (some claim), men are more likely to shoot rock, while women are more likely to shoot scissors. This also means that paper is habitually undershot. So shoot rock—it beats the feminine scissors, while remaining safe due to paper's improbability.

But everyone knows this and so rock has the reputation as the choice of rookies.

If, before you started playing, you inserted into your explanation of RPS strategy the phrase "rock is for rookies," you'd be priming your opponent *not* to shoot rock. Having done this, you could shoot scissors knowing it would win or tie. The crux is accurately evaluating your opponent's skill level.

Now, a clever man would put the poison into his own goblet, because he would know that only a great fool would reach for what he was given. I am not a great fool, so I can clearly not choose the wine in front of you. But you must have known I was not a great fool, you would have counted on it, so I can clearly not choose the wine in front of me.

—Vizzini, *The Princess Bride*

THE HEDONOMETER

Are you feeling the wanderlust of mist blue or the rejuvenation of deep teal? What about the romance of amethyst or the turbulent mood shifts of firebrick?

Everyone knows that the color of your ring shows your emotion. OK, maybe not *everyone*. Skeptics include mathematician Peter Dodds and computer scientist Chris Danforth, who work in the Advanced Computing Center at the University of Vermont. Their skepticism led them to design a measurement for happiness *even more accurate* than the mood ring(!). They call it the hedonometer.

First, their software (www.wefeelfine.org) crawled more than 2.3 million blogs looking for sentences that begin with "I am feeling" or "I feel." And because a large study known as Affective Norms for English Words had already assigned words certain happiness scores ("paradise" gets 8.72, "suicide" gets 1.25, "pancakes" gets 6.08), Dodds and Danforth were able to put a happiness value on each sentence. Sure there were some false happy hits, but by averaging enough sentences from enough blogs, Dodds and Danforth effectively slapped a mood ring on the Internet.

So, how happy are we?

Well, crawling online music databases shows that lyrics got decidedly less chipper from the '60s to the '90s. Interestingly, though, it's new song genres that drove the downward spiral, while lyrics within genres

---

The only thing better than technology that measures mood is technology that *creates* it. For example, BrainWave, an iPhone app featuring "scientifically engineered binaural frequency programs designed to synchronize the frequency of your brain waves with that of your designed state of mind." Simulate morning coffee, euphoria, lucid dreaming, and more, all for ninety-nine cents. Or try the app Live Happy, by UC Riverside professor Sonja Lyubomirsky, which guides users through daily happiness exercises.

stayed stable (think the Monkees versus Marilyn Manson). And using the demographics of blog authors, Dodds and Danforth found a happiness belt running through the Earth's temperate latitudes. They also found proof of teen angst, showing a spike in the under-twenty use of words like "hate", "sick," "stupid," and "fat." On the flip side, there was a massive spike in the word "proud" on November 4, 2008.

LOGIC OF ILLOGIC: BRAIN-DEFLATING FALLACIES TO WIN ANY ARGUMENT, PART I

Use the following strategies to ensure dominance in debate club and/or with an unsuspecting significant other.

• Appeal to ignorance: if it isn't proven, it's false. *"Did you SEE me bogart the last of the jamocha almond fudge? No? Well, there you go."*

• Ad hominem: Discrediting an argument by discrediting the person making it. *"I am right because you suck."*

• Affirming the consequent: If x, then y. Y, therefore x. *"When you're wrong you get defensive. Oooh, oooh, you're getting defensive. You're wrong! I win!"*

• Argument to logic: If an argument offered is false, then the entire claim is false. *"Actually, that's not my spoon in the sink! Thus am I exonerated!"*

• Loaded question: Any answer validates an assumption. *"Why must you always persecute me unjustly?"*

EYE HACK: GRAVITY HILL

If a car were sitting where the kids are standing, would it roll toward you or away? Duh, you know it's an optical illusion, so the car must roll away. But that's pretty freaky, huh? Because *most* foothills slope up toward the mountains, our brain expects these foothills to do the same. Nope. The keys to this illusion are a mostly obscured horizon and lack of trees or other vertical visual clues. This downward slope as upward slope illusion is known as a gravity hill. A quick Internet search returns the locations of hundreds of gravity hills around the world.

THE CALCULUS OF COMPASSION

You see a person mugged in the middle of a crowded city block. You come upon a motorist stuck on the side of a rural road. Your boss makes a racist joke in the lunchroom. A bag breaks and a harried dad's groceries spill onto the sidewalk.

Do you act? It depends on how your brain calculates the costs.

A classic study by psychologists John Darley and Bibb Latané found that the more witnesses there are to an event, the less likely any one person is to help. This, they said, is because the responsibility for the person in need is spread over all the onlookers. If you were to help, your individual costs in terms of time, effort, risk, etc., would outweigh the fraction of the total responsibility that is yours. This means that a motorist may have a much more difficult time flagging down help on the side of a busy freeway than he might on the Alaska Highway. In the first case, a passing driver can expect that someone else will stop; in the second case, the responsibility is on one driver alone.

But lest ye prematurely chalk humans up as cold, cold machines, don't forget to factor empathy into the calculus of compassion. The more connection you feel with the person in distress, the more it costs you to simply walk past. Thus when a harried dad spills his groceries on the sidewalk, another dad would be most likely to stop. (And with more people watching, there's more likely to be another dad in the audience—so a crowd's increased chance of including one person who empathizes may outweigh the decreased overall responsibility of each person in the crowd.)

What about the crime in broad daylight? There are many

potential costs of action. Again, costs include risk, time, and effort. And there are risks of inaction: guilt, blame, further crimes. (Can you plausibly deny knowledge that a crime occurred right in front of you? Can you assume the police will catch the perpetrator without your help?) And there are the rewards of heroism, both external and internal.

The values of these factors create our choice.

And they do it in a blink. In the second before whizzing past, we notice if the hitchhiker is a derelict or simply a distressed motorist just like us (empathy). We notice if the pickpocket looks dangerous (risk). We evaluate how likely the problem is to be solved without our help (responsibility). We think of the $500 for returning the lost dog to the attractive lady (rewards).

Our brain runs the numbers and then we act. Or we don't.

GAME THEORY MAKE BRAIN BIG: THE ORIGIN OF FAIRNESS

In a classic experiment known as the Ultimatum Game, person

For rather depressing examples of human inaction, do a quick online search for the phrase "bystander apathy."

A is given 10 coins to split between himself and person B. If person B accepts the distribution, they both keep the coins; if not, no one gets paid. According to Game Theory, the optimal solution is for person A to give himself nine coins and person B one coin—both will end the game richer than when they started. However, played in the wild, the most common distribution is 6-to-4, a ratio seen as fair by both parties.

But why? What's the origin of the human idea of fairness?

To answer that, let's take a look at a spin on the Ultimatum Game called the Dictator Game. In Dictator, player A decides how to split the 10 coins and they're split accordingly. Just like that. Player B has no say. In *this* game, person A is much more likely to split the coins 9-to-1.

The difference between Ultimatum and Dictator is, of course, person B's ability to punish person A. Let's take a closer look:

In Ultimatum, person B scoffs at a one-coin offer, sacrificing personal gain in order to punish person A's greed. Game theorists call this move an *altruistic punishment*. While person B loses a coin in this maneuver, he can expect his corrective behavior to result in more coins for him and all the other Bs of the world down the line.

Over time, player A has come to expect punishment for unfair behavior and has learned to limit his greed. So to some extent, humans have become *social maximizers* instead of *personal maximizers*.

Unfortunately for the mass singing of kumbaya and the potential dawning of a modern Aquarian age, this implies that human fairness is borne of player A's fear of reprisal and player B's angling for future payoff, and not of any innate higher moral order.

Autistic people, who tend to lack awareness of social norms, are the only players likely to suggest a 9-to-1 split in the Ultimatum Game. They are also the only players likely to accept this split.

SELF-TEST

Read the following statements and use a pencil to score each question's accuracy in describing your thoughts or behaviors, with one being "very inaccurate" and five being "very accurate." Flip to the back of the book for interpretation.

1. I like to be of service to others.

2. I distrust people.

3. I am nice to store clerks.

4. I acknowledge others' accomplishments.

5. I pretend to be concerned for others.

6. I can't be bothered with others' needs.

7. I try to maintain a pleasant atmosphere.

8. I disregard the opinions of others.

The Smell of Trust

Imagine the following trust game: An "investor" has 12 coins, and can give any number of them to a "trustee." Any coins given quadruple in value, and then the trustee can give back as many (or as few) as he or she wants. Thus it's best for the investor to give coins, but only if the investor trusts the trustee.

Researchers in Zurich added a hitch: Half the tested pairs inhaled a placebo nasal spray and half inhaled a spray containing oxytocin, a drug linked to long-term mating and nurturing behaviors. In the placebo pairs, only one-fifth of investors forked over all their coins; in the oxytocin pairs, almost half did. Oxytocin had no influence on the number of coins trustees returned, perhaps because no trust was required on their end of the transaction.

WILD KINGDOM: MARTYRDOM IN BREWER'S YEAST

If the goal of life is to pass on one's genes, why are some animals willing to take a hit for the good of the group?

William D. Hamilton answered this question by imagining a population in which some of its members have a gene that codes for green beards. In this population, when a person with a green beard helps another green beard, they ensure the continuation of the green-beard gene. The individual may not act in his own best interest, but he acts in the best interest of his genome. (If your actions save ten people, each of whom shares 10 percent of your unique genes, you've balanced your own life.)

We see this phenomenon in brewer's yeast. At the end of fermentation, the yeasty little buggers have created enough alcohol to make their surroundings toxic. And so they clump together in impenetrable balls, sacrificing the yeast at the ball's outer edge as a shield against the poison. By their sacrifice, the outer yeast ensure the survival of the genetically similar inner yeast.

In another (more violent) example, fire ant queens of genes bb, Bb, or BB have different smells. Queens who are bb die off naturally. Fire ant workers who are Bb kill off queens who are BB, leaving only Bb queens to reproduce, thereby ensuring the continuation of their own Bb worker genome.

The brain of an ant is one of the most marvellous atoms of matter in the world, perhaps more so than the brain of a man.

—Charles Darwin

MAD PRIDE

I am Napoleon. What, you don't believe me? Oh I see, all of a sudden you get all *superior* just because your opinion happens to represent "society."

Well you can have August through June, but July is my month. That's right: July is Mad Pride Month, with July 14 being Mad Pride Day. If you're bipolar, obsessive compulsive, a kleptomaniac, a hypochondriac, schizophrenic, or otherwise touched, please join me in July for parading, speechifying, and other assorted mad gallantry in cities around the globe.

I'll be riding a horse and wearing a very stylish hat. You can follow me.

HEAR WITH YOUR EYES, SPEAK WITH YOUR EARS

Neuroscientist David Ostry designed a mouth-stretching robot. When it pulled subjects' lips up, they interpreted a computerized voice as saying "head."

Zen Mind

A monk asked Joshu, "I've heard that you personally met Nansen. Is it true or not?" Joshu replied, "The province of Chin produces giant radishes."

When the robot pulled their lips down, the subjects interpreted the identical sound as "had." Why? These robo-genic lip positions mimic the shapes we use to speak these words, and the shape of our mouth influences what we hear.

And your ears? It turns out they speak too. And not only when spoken to. The ear actually emits sounds, sometimes loud enough to be heard without special instruments.

Try it: find a quiet room and a willing partner and sit ear-to-ear. See what happens.

But What Do the Voices Say?

Psychologists encourage us to listen to and interpret our dreams—why not do the same for the voices of schizophrenia? British psychologist Rufus May leads Hearing Voices Network groups, in which he encourages schizophrenics to explore and learn from what their voices are saying. This, May hopes, will help schizophrenics apply the same real/unreal judgments we make with dreams.

Signals from the ear hit the brain in the temporal lobe, specifically in the primary auditory cortex of the left temporal lobe. Here, we process the signals of speech and store our vocabularies. And to some extent, the right temporal lobe controls how we use this speech. And so damage to the left temporal lobe can affect the ability to interpret and create speech, while damage to the right temporal lobe can remove the governor that decides how much speech is appropriate (see San Francisco mayor Gavin Newsom's 2008 seven-plus-hour state of the city address).

The right temporal lobe also stores our list of faces, and so damage can result in prosopagnosia, or face blindness, as this list becomes detached from the faces it represents. Perhaps because a damaged temporal lobe struggles to interpret sound information, many people with temporal lobe damage experience cross-modal sensory experiences, including "hearing colors."

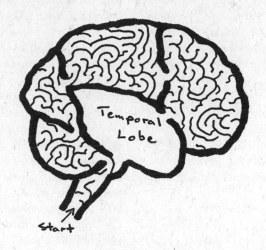

Start

PSY-OP: FLEXIBLE MIND OF MASTERY

First solve these practice problems (don't try looking in the back—the answers aren't there):

• Problem #1: You have three jars. Jar A holds 9 units of water, jar B holds 40 units, and jar C holds 2 units. How can you measure exactly 20 units?

• Problem #2: Jar A holds 32 units, jar B holds 90 units, and jar C holds 4 units. How can you measure 50 units?

• Problem #3: Jar A holds 21 units, jar B holds 127 units, and jar C holds 3 units. How can you measure exactly 100 units?

Now solve this test problem:

• Test: Jar A holds 6 units, jar B holds 78 units, and jar C holds 22 units. How can you measure 28 units?

Chances are, you started with 78, subtracted 2-times-22, and then subtracted another 6 (B − 2C − A). That's the technique you learned by doing those three practice problems. But there's another solution: just add 22 and 6 (A + C).

Don't feel stupid. This water jar experiment by Abraham Luchins (1942) is a classic demonstration of the Einstellung effect: Your previous experience makes the new problem more difficult.

And the Einstellung effect isn't confined to water jars. It leaps the laboratory, showing up in situations like chess. We apply the solutions that worked in the past even when better solutions are available.

Or, certain people do.

To have previous solutions to fall back on requires some exper- tise. And so experts fall into the Einstellung trap: They use familiar, nonoptimal solutions (while nonexperts—with less expertise— use new, nonoptimal solutions).

But something interesting happens when chess players reach a certain level of expertise: they stop getting sucked into the Einstellung trap. At the stage of Zen chess enlightenment, the mind again becomes as flexible as the uncarved block, and masters look past familiarity and into optimal solutions, be they in or out of the box.

Neurological Explanation of the Einstellung Effect

Why do we fall back on the familiar ways we've done things, even when these solutions aren't the best? One explanation is neuroplasticity: Over time, you physically rewire your brain for this solution.

Here's how it works: Neurons that play together stay together. Or, neurons in a pathway that fire together learn to fire together more efficiently. This pathway becomes quicker on a basic, biological level. And so this pathway beats out other, competing pathways, even when the other pathways might have been naturally quicker before all the rewiring started.

INMATES RUNNING THE PRISON: INSANE RULERS

While the inbred Europeans of the middle ages take the prize for sheer volume of madness (Henry VI, Joanna of Castille, Charles II of Spain, Maria I of Portugal, etc., etc., etc.), the Romans have them beat on a case-by-case basis for the whimsical expression of tyrannical insanity.

Whack jobs don't get much wackier than the Roman emperor Caligula, who ruled from A.D. 37–41. Anecdotes include incest with and pimping of his sisters, forcing his father-in-law to commit suicide, and making his horse, Incitatus, a consul and priest.

Justin II, emperor of Byzantium from A.D. 565–578, attempted to bluff his Persian enemies using the eastern empire's waning power. It didn't work and the strain left him insane in the membrane. After abdication he took to being wheeled through the palace, biting (and sometimes eating) attendants to the soundtrack of organ music.

Ibrahim I was Sultan of the Ottoman Empire from A.D. 1640–1648. He liked big women. In fact, he scoured the empire for the biggest woman in the world, finally bringing to the palace a 330-pound Armenian whom he nicknamed Sugar Cube. When a rumor reached him that his harem had been untrue, he had 280 concubines drowned in the Bosporus Sea.

Joanna of Castille loved her husband, Philip the Handsome. She continued to love him even after his death—so much so that she brought his corpse with her on a tour of Europe.

Charles VI, known as Charles the Mad, was prone to "episodes." In one, he charged and killed four of his knights. At a feast, he and four others dressed up as wild men and covered themselves in oil. Of course, they caught fire and all but the mad king were killed. He saved himself by jumping under a lady's long train.

Christian VII of Denmark suffered from paranoia and hallucinations, and enjoyed roaming through the streets beating subjects with a spiked mace and having himself stretched on the rack and flogged.

Was Ludwig II of Bavaria insane or just eccentric? Who knows? We do know that he championed the music of Richard Wagner and bankrupted his fortune commissioning fairy-tale castles like Schloss Neuschwanstein (neither the act of a sane man).

PERSIAN COW PRINCE

Around the year A.D. 1000, a Persian prince became convinced he was a cow. The prince wouldn't eat, mooed, and cried, "Kill me so that a good stew may be made of my flesh!" He was brought to the great Arabic doctor Ibn Sina, who held a sharp knife, had the prince lay on the floor as if for slaughter, and said, "The cow is too lean and not ready to be killed. He must be fed properly and I will kill it when it becomes healthy and fat." The cow prince eagerly ate, and with food came strength and his delusion was cured.

Ibn Sina is considered one of the forefathers of Western psychoanalysis.

LOGIC OF ILLOGIC: BRAIN-DEFLATING FALLACIES TO WIN ANY ARGUMENT, PART II

Still more strategies to ensure dominance in debate club and/or with an unsuspecting significant other:

- Denying the antecedent: If x, then y. Not x. Therefore not y. *"If I had fudge on my chin, you'd know I bogarted the very last of the jamocha almond fudge. Do you see said fudge? No. Thus am I exonerated!"*

- Disjunctive fallacy: X and/or y. Not x. Therefore not y. *"So, I see you accuse both me and the dog. But in fact the dog is allergic to chocolate! Thus am I exonerated!"*

- Division fallacy: Assuming that all individuals posses characteristics of the group (this is stereotypical stereotyping). *"It's in the nature of a middle-aged woman to bogart the very last of the jamocha almond fudge. Thus you, my dear wife—and not I—have done exactly that."*

- Existential fallacy: Are there any members in that category? *"Standing before you are all the people who have not bogarted the very last of the jamocha almond fudge. You are the only other suspect. Thus, j'accuse!"*

- False analogy: A misleading comparison. *"Gandhi, a man similar to myself in many respects, wouldn't have bogarted the last of the jamocha almond fudge."*

THE EXPRESSIVE BODY

The science of body language goes far beyond dating tips (FYI: touch your collarbone, mimic his or her movements, be conspicuous, show interest). For example, researchers showed forty male tennis players video of other tennis players warming up. Then subjects watched these players in action. Regardless of the players' actual performance during match play, subjects assigned higher skill levels to players who showed strong body language during their warm-ups. And subjects were pessimistic about their own chances against the players who projected strength and competence before even picking up a racket. Because confidence breeds success in tennis (and in many other activities), the body language of the warm-up affects the outcome of the match.

In fact, our body language is so definitive that even a computer can recognize its meaning. Researchers hooked a computer to subjects' visual cortexes allowing the computer to recognize brain patterns that showed how subjects held their bodies. Based on this information alone, the computer was able to accurately predict subjects' emotional states.

But body language is not simply a tool that unintentionally outs our emotions. Instead, it's a valuable component of our ability to communicate. When you hear speech, mirror neurons in your brain map this speech onto motor circuits that you would use if you were producing this speech. For example, when you hear the word "ball" you briefly imagine how it would feel to say this word. This test helps you interpret the word's meaning. Researchers showed this by having subjects listen to the Italian words *"birra"* and *"buffo."* Why those words? Saying the first word requires moving the tongue; saying the second doesn't. When subjects heard *"birra,"* their motor cortexes showed more activity in the area that prepares and produces tongue movement. We imagine saying what we hear.

And speech accompanied by gesture actually allows the speech-recognition area of the brain (Broca's area) to chill out a bit. Researchers showed that when we see gestures, our mirror neurons fire and then we gather meaning directly from the mirror neurons—circumventing Broca's area. In other words, speaking with gestures allows direct communication between motor circuits, leaving Broca's area free to focus on only speech.

What's interesting about all these studies (yes, including the dating tips) is that they imply a whole-brain construction of meaning. And, on a basic neurological level, this meaning consists both of what we say and what we do.

SHORT AND STOUT, LONG AND TALL

Which of the glasses in this topic's doodle holds more liquid?

Before blowing the answer, check this out:

Researchers at a teen health and fitness camp found that teens given short-wide glasses poured 76 percent more juice than those given tall-slender glasses. And despite this, the stout-glassed group *believed* they'd actually poured and drank less juice.

Experienced bartenders fall into the same trap: an ounce in a wide shot is bigger than an ounce in a tall shot. Oh, and in the illustration above, the short glass holds almost double the liquid of the tall glass (remember volume = $\pi r^2 h$ and so a cup's radius is a much bigger deal than its height).

Eye Hack: Which Is Longer, Segment AB or Segment BC?

Because you know this is an eye hack, you might've guessed they're the same length (really, they are). But our brains see this parallelogram as a tilted rectangle and ABC as a tilted right triangle with unequal sides.

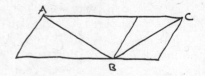

Why, outside of trivia, does this matter?

Parents or dieticians can exploit the short-stout effect to trick their wards into drinking more healthy beverages. And restaurants can and do exploit tall, thin glasses when serving four-buck-a-cup fresh-squeezed orange juice.

PIECE OF MIND: HYPOTHALAMUS

The hypothalamus is a way station where input becomes output. Specifically, it accepts smells, electrical signals, and blood-borne signals, and then based on these stimuli releases corresponding hormones (or prods the pituitary into releasing hormones).

A cool example of the hypothalamus linking input and output is seen in mice. After she mates with a male, a female mouse may run across a new male mouse in the course of her daily scufflings. Is he studlier than her previous mate? If so, she may choose to hang around him (or his droppings or urine), thereby inhaling his manly rodent odor. And this scent of a strange male, soon after mating, induces the mouse hypothalamus to release a hormone that aborts her developing pregnancy. Within one to four days, she'll be in estrus and able to mate with the new George Clooney-mouse.

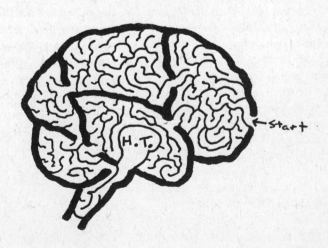

Interestingly, the hypothalamus also regulates food intake. Cranking up the hypothalamus's activity creates overeating and obesity. And a mute hypothalamus can stop a creature's food intake entirely.

Genius Tester #1:
Well Hung

On Monday, a prisoner sits in a cell waiting to be hanged. He is told he will be executed before the weekend but that he won't know the day of his execution beforehand. He reasons that if he were to be hung on Friday, he could deduce this from being alive on Thursday night. So Friday's out. But if Friday's out and he's alive on Wednesday night, he can deduce that he must be hung on Thursday. And since he can't know the day beforehand, Thursday's out. He works back through the week and realizes he cannot be executed. And so he is unpleasantly surprised when he is hung on Tuesday.

What went wrong?

LOGIC OF ILLOGIC: ANCHORING

MBA students at MIT's Sloan School of Management are an analytical group—expert in pricing theory—and should be paragons of economic rationality. But when researchers asked two groups of students to bid on the same goods (chocolate and wine) they were able to get one group to bid 60 to 120 percent more than the other.

How?

Blame it on their social security numbers. Professor Dan Ariely asked MBA students to write down the last two digits of their social security numbers before submitting bids. Those with higher digits submitted higher bids.

This is known as *anchoring*. The social security numbers provided students with an unconscious starting point—either a high or a low anchor—which they then adjusted, but never fully overcame, when evaluating the products themselves.

Of course, marketing professionals would never dream of exploiting anchoring to make us overpay for goods. Consider: "How much would you pay for this set of knives? Three hundred dollars? Two hundred dollars? Well today, it's available to you for the one-time price of thirty-nine ninety-five!" Because we're anchored to $300, $39.95 sounds like a steal.

Or consider the iPhone, initially priced at $599. That's steep for a cell phone. The *Washington Post* quotes aforementioned econ guru Dan Ariely saying of the phone's initial price, "It establishes a reference price of $600, and now when it comes down . . . we compare it to the higher price. I don't know if Steve Jobs planned this or not, but if he manipulated based on anchoring, he did a very nice trick." And not only does the $599 anchor make a still-steep $399 iPhone look like a steal, but the high price signals its value.

OUIJA TWEET BRAIN INTERFACE

The responsibility of Twitter updates got you down? D'you think about tweeting but never actually get around to it? Never fear, Adam Wilson is here. The University of Wisconsin–Madison biomedical engineering grad student removes the clunky and outdated interface of keyboard and lets his brain tweet for him. That's right, he straps an electrode-coated swim cap to his head and watches as letters scroll across his computer screen. When his brain recognizes the letter he wants, the swim cap knows and uploads it directly to Twitter. What's the meaning of that F to which you're inexplicably drawn? Why does your attention keep traveling toward the S? Now, thanks to Adam Wilson, you can become conscious of your unconscious, and make sure everyone else in the Tweetosphere is conscious of it too.

Genius Tester #2: Bridge and Torch

Four people come to a narrow bridge at night. Between them, they have one torch, which has to be carried in order for anyone to cross. Only two people can cross the bridge at a time. Person A can cross the bridge in 1 minute, B in 2 minutes, C in 5 minutes, and D in 8 minutes. When two people cross the bridge together, they go at the slower person's pace. How can they all cross the bridge in 15 minutes or less?

ALGEBRAIC EIGHT-BALL: AT WHAT AGE WILL TECHNOLOGY OVERTAKE YOUR ABILITY TO USE IT?

- A = Your current age.

- S_N = On how many of the following services are you a registered user? Facebook, MySpace, Friendster, Twitter, Blogger, Badoo, Bebo, Flickr, LinkedIn.

- C_T = How many cell phones do you own?

- D = In how many of the following dinosaur activities do you participate on a daily basis: read the newspaper, subscribe to a newspaper, use a pen/pencil, watch TV, listen to music that has ever been placed on any nondigital recordable media, recreate off-line.

- W = In how many programming languages could you design a widget of any sort?

- P = How many of the following people have you heard of? Linus Torvalds, Ray Ozzie, Kevin Mitnick, Jean Grey, Samwise Gamgee, Violet Blue.

$$A + \frac{(S_N + C_T + W + P)^2}{\sqrt{D+2}} = A_{TECH}$$

A_{TECH} is the age at which your human operating system will become outdated. Notice that you may not have much time.

DEBUNKED: SELF-AFFIRMATION STINKS

Do you ever get insecure? Feel blue? Feel like a worthless jet of penguin goo? Try this famous affirmation by Al Franken's *SNL* character Stuart Smalley: "I'm good enough, I'm smart enough, and doggone it, people like me." Repeat it until you believe it.

Actually, don't.

A 2009 study published in the journal *Psychological Science* found that self-affirmations make people with low self-esteem feel worse. People with high self-esteem benefit little if at all.

THE ECONOMICS OF MATING I: MONOGAMY, POLYGAMY, AND POLYAMORY

Despite the noise of the information age, at the end of the day, humans still want to pass on our genes. But while it takes men between three and thirty minutes to do so, it takes women nine months (plus nursing, etc., etc.). And so a man's reproductive potential is bound by the number of mates he can find, while a woman's reproductive success is bound by the time/energy it takes to successfully raise her children.

And so the sexes battle: Genetically, men want more mates and women want help. And historically, resources decide the winner.

In cultures that evolved in resource-rich areas, females didn't need male help to raise their children. Thus they gave little preference to males who would stick around to share the burden. These males, unfettered by paternal investment, quickly went in search of additional mates, but supply and demand meant they needed to fight for them—males in polyamorous so-cieties tend to be big and horny, as it were.

But in resource-poor environments, women needed the contribution of hunting men, and it

Boys Have Cooties

Due to the evolutionary pressures of male competition and selection for better hunters, most male mammals are larger than their female counterparts. A bigger body makes a better lunch for discerning parasites, and thus most male mammals have higher rates of parasitic infection.

was all a dude could do to put enough meat on the table to feed a single family. Thus monogamy and paternal investment.

And finally, in societies in which men had access to resources while women did not, polygamy developed—women needed (or were forced to need) male resources in order to raise their children, and certain men could supply these in enough quantity to support many women.

This is of course a vast oversimplification of a fiendishly complicated and much-debated topic. For a proper discussion, check out *The Mating Mind* by Geoffrey Miller.

PARASITE BRAIN PUNK

The very good WNYC program *Radiolab* describes the journey of the parasite *Toxoplasma gondii*. Said parasite wants to breed inside the guts of cats. But after breeding, toxo—along with the other contents of cats' guts—tends to end up in the litter box or beneath your neighbor's hedge. What happens to expelled cat poop? Well, in a stunningly lovely visual, much of it's eaten by rats. So now, the excreted toxo is living inside rats . . . and it wants to get back into the cat so that it can reproduce.

How does it do this?

Toxoplasma gondii migrates from the rat's gut to its brain, where it invades the amygdala and snips the rat's fear response to the smell of cat pee. In fact, not only does it turn off the fear of cat smell, but it connects this snipped wire with the area that controls sexual arousal: Now the rat is hot for cats.

This is not good for the rat. Soon it ends up in the cat's belly, where *T. gondii* can continue the never-ending circle of life.

Here's the thing: *Toxoplasma gondii* can live in humans too. And when we eat cat poop (unintentionally, one would hope) or scratch ourselves with something crusted with cat feces (same), we give it the chance to enter our bodies. How does *Toxoplasma gondii* know it's in a human and not in a rat? Well, it doesn't. And so it migrates to our brains, where it bounces around looking for trouble.

Does toxo make us like cats? Maybe. There's clinical conjecture, if not outright support, for toxo's contribution to the stereotypical crazy cat lady. And there's definitely clinical confirmation of the crazy part: *Toxo-*

plasma gondii is a proven risk factor for schizophrenia (and cases of schizophrenia bloomed in the 1800s, along with the practice of keeping cats as pets—coincidence?).

There's also evidence that, like in rats, *Toxoplasma gondii* decreases our experience of fear: it's been shown to be a risk factor in traffic accidents, implying that toxo-infected drivers are reckless.

HANG UP AND DRIVE: YOUR BRAIN, SPLIT

It makes sense: If you hold a phone, you have only one hand for the steering wheel; if you dial, you look away from the road. But studies show that the effects of driving while yakking go beyond difficult auto mechanics (as it were). In fact, fMRI studies show that talking on the cell while driving makes the brain itself a dumber driver.

The brain's parietal lobe is responsible for spatial processing and generally knows if you are or aren't going to messily whack something with a Buick (it's also responsible for high Tetris scores). But the brain drain of talking on the cell while driving results in less parietal lobe activation (a 37 percent decrease, according to one study).

It's as if our brain is a city with rolling blackouts: We can't power everything at once, and if energy goes to cell conversation, it's taken away from driving.

So is multitasking a tool of the devil, leading to the devolution of the brain and the loss of human planetary dominance? A study published in the journal *Science* says yes (OK, they didn't quite put it that way).

Researchers compared heavy media multitaskers (computer,

iDread

Nomophobia: fear of being out of mobile-phone coverage.

Genius Tester #3: Meeting in the Middle

Imagine you're going on vacation and your mother has agreed to watch your Labrador. You live an hour's drive apart. At 7:30 a.m., you'll both start driving toward each other and will exchange the dog wherever you meet in the middle, presumably around 8:00 at the exact midpoint. But you'd *really* like to get back to your house as soon as possible. Should you leave a little earlier or later than 7:30? Should you drive fast or slow? What's your best driving strategy to get you home ASAP?

music, web, texting, talking—all at once), to light media multitaskers and found that even when unplugged, the heavy media group was worse at filtering relevant information from the environment, worse at quickly retrieving relevant information from their memories, and worse at quickly switching cognitive tasks.

These results are far from conclusive—much more research is needed—but they suggest that rather than training the brain for this brave, new, media-rich world, multitasking makes us less suited for pretty much everything.

THE ECONOMICS OF MATING II: SNEAKY FEMALE REGULATION OF THE FREE MARKET

Imagine the ideal reproductive circumstances for women: male competition and paternal investment amid enough resources to ensure their children's survival. Hmmm, this sounds vaguely familiar. Wait a minute! This is modern society, in which men spend resources parenting when they could be off further procreating.

In short, men have been biologically bamboozled. But how?

Economically, the first step is regulation of the free market. Morality performs the role of the SEC, dictating that men enter monogamous relationships even though such relationships hamper male reproductive potential. At least this pesky morality increases paternal certainty, allowing men to be fairly sure that the children in whom they are overinvesting are their own.

So that's monogamy out of the way, but morality can't explain it all: With exactly enough mates to go around, men shouldn't need to butt heads, lock antlers, build bowers, or otherwise compete for female attention. What then of football? And of Gold's Gym and singles bars and law school?

It turns out that female *Homo sapiens* are tricky and have developed the behavioral ability to combat the natural laws of the universe. Specifically, women have become picky and wary of casual sex that could cause pregnancy. Men, you may have noticed that most women will not mate with just anyone. Instead, women hold their reproductive cards tightly, and will show their hands only to men of their choosing. This forces men to compete even for the opportunity to mate with just one woman! And women use the power of choice to maximize their reproductive potential by wisely choosing men who demonstrate the potential for paternal investment.

WILD KINGDOM: HUMMINGBIRDS VS. FIGHTER PILOTS

Let's admit it's more than a stereotype: ladies like fighter pilots. Maybe it's the pilots' ability to swoop and dive and generally blow other males out of the sky (with overtly Freudian weaponry).

At least that's what lights a lady hummingbird's lamp.

After flapping his wings to initiate a courtship dive, the male hummingbird folds into a missile, reaching speeds of 385 body lengths per second. That's the equivalent of an F-22 Raptor flying at approximately 15,400 mph or about Mach 20 (ten times faster than the super fighter's top speed). When the fighter jock hummingbird slams on the breaks, he pulls nine G's, tops in the animal kingdom.

Can you say "Take me to bed or lose me forever"?

COOL NEUROSURGERY PAST AND PRESENT: PREFRONTAL LOBOTOMY

If personality's a problem, why not turn it off? That's what neurosurgeons did in the United States, Great Britain, and throughout Scandinavia, mostly from the 1930s to 1950s. And it was pretty simple: once personality was (correctly) blamed on the prefrontal cortex, all neurosurgeons had to do was to snip all the wires into and out of it.

In the United States, the prefrontal lobotomy was pioneered by Walter Freeman, who hoped it could be used on a shoestring budget and without anesthesia in state mental hospitals (using existing electroshock facilities to render patients unconscious during the surgery). Because by licensure only neurosurgeons were allowed to drill holes in the skull and because state mental hospitals were unlikely to have access to a neurosurgeon, Freeman hit on the bright idea of accessing the brain through the eye sockets. Basically, he slid a long metal object along the path of the upper eyelid and then gave it a solid smack with a hammer to drive it through the thin layer of bone covering the brain.

His tool of choice was an ice pick.

Once inside, he waggled the pick back and forth to cut the connection between the prefrontal lobe and the thalamus. He then repeated the procedure on the other side.

About 40,000 people in the United States had their prefrontal cortexes nixed from the system, including Rosemary Kennedy (JFK's sister), who was lobotomized as a twenty-three-year-old due to "moodiness." The procedure left her incontinent and unable to speak.

Luckily, lobotomies went out of vogue with the advent of thorazine and then other antipsychotic drugs.

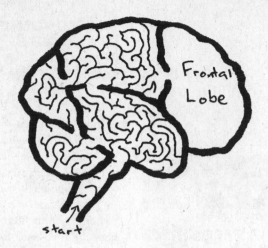

start

PIECE OF MIND: FRONTAL LOBE

Pulling a bike helmet down to just above your eyebrows protects the frontal lobe. And woe be unto ye who smack the frontal lobe, as it is the home of our ability to predict the future. As such, a smacked frontal lobe makes for a poor gambler: If someone with damaged frontal lobes pulls nine white socks out of a drawer of ten white socks and ten black socks, he may still predict the tenth sock is equally likely to be black or white. So too, telling a person with misfiring frontal lobes that the Patriots have pulverized the Lions in every game since the departure of Barry Sanders does little to affect their estimation of the point spread (for this reason, it's sometimes hard to distinguish the predictions of die-hard Lions fans from those of patients with damaged frontal lobes).

In fact, lesion of the right frontal lobe has been shown to remove the ability to make any decisions based on advice. Even with inside information that the Patriots will beat the Lions, a frontal-lobe-less gambler may put his money on the Lions.

The frontal lobe also allows us to predict the outcomes of our own actions: What's the likely outcome of hitting that snowboard kicker at 40 mph? What might happen if you have just one more beer? What's the result of an affair? It's as if removing the influence of the frontal lobe releases our id, which can result in basic personality changes.

Wild Kingdom: The Red-Necked Phalarope

In exceptional societies like that of the red-necked phalarope, in which males raise the offspring, male reproductive potential is bound by time and energy, and female reproductive potential is bound by the number of mates she can find. Fittingly, female red-necked phalaropes compete for males and then guard their men jealously.

THE ECONOMICS OF MATING III: FEMALE COMPETITION

According to the rules of good old Darwinian free-market ecology, women should be able to sit back (with their legs tightly crossed and/or their birth control firmly in place) and wait for suitors to come suiting. But the female finagling that leads to male competition skews the 50/50 balance of mates and means that females need to compete to be competed for. (English translation: women fight for the most suitable suitors.)

This isn't always pretty.

But unlike men, who prefer whacking one another with sticks, the major model of the modern major female reproductive competition is to exclude opponents from social groups that ensure successful mating. This, in a nutshell, is why it sucks to be a middle-school girl.

Eye Hack: Che Lives!

Stare at Che. Keep staring. Now quickly look at a piece of blank, white paper (or another white surface). You should see an afterimage in which Che's hat and beard are black. The effect is due to the photoreceptors in your eyes being overtaxed by the original image. The white overwhelms, and so the cone cells compensate by toning it down. If they're dialing white toward black and you take away the picture, the white areas that are dialed down appear blacker than their surroundings.

LOGIC OF ILLOGIC: BATTLE ROBOT

Imagine it's 1963 and you're a kid sitting in a playroom with a totally kick-ass battle robot toy in front of you. Now imagine that a bunch of dudes in white coats leave you alone with the robot . . . but before they do so, they forbid you to play with it. In fact, they say you'll be severely punished if you so much as touch it again. (They tell other kids in other rooms that they'll only be *moderately* punished if they play with the robot.)

iDread

Bolshephobia: fear of Bolsheviks.

Amazingly, both you and the "moderately punished" kids are able to keep your hands off the 'bot. Then the white coats say *just kidding:* You can all play with the robot again!

Of the kids threatened with severe or moderate punishment, only one group returns to playing with the robot. Which do you think it is? You'd think the kids who were threatened with severe punishment would still be scared to play with the 'bot, right? Right?

Actually, it's the other way around. When threat of punishment is removed, kids in the "severe" group go right back to the 'bot, while kids in the "moderate" punishment group tend to favor other toys.

This is because the threat of severe punishment was enough reason for kids to stop playing with the robot, while the threat of moderate punishment wasn't enough in itself to keep kids away. These "moderate" kids had to augment the threat of punishment with their own reasons to stay away. They devalued the robot or otherwise rationalized their decision not to play with it—reasons that lingered even after the threat of punishment was removed.

WILD KINGDOM: RECREATIONAL RAT PHARMA- COPEIA

Rats like to party. This from a study of opium, alcohol, amphetamines, psilocybin, nicotine, and cannabis use in rodents. Specifically, any one drug acted as a gateway for others. For example, rats who smoked pot (clinically speaking) more highly self-administered heroin when given the chance (and vice versa all the way around the circle). Were test subjects released into the wild? Did they form bands and join the Bonnaroo festival circuit? Did researchers fail to notice the data potential of Keith Richards?

Regardless, once the brain gets a taste of artificially generated dopamine release, it's likely to look for more of the same in the future—no matter the source.

PIECE OF MIND: MIDBRAIN

Also known as the mesencephalon, the midbrain is the home of addiction. Usually, the midbrain (specifically a structure within it called the substantia nigra) kicks out carefully regulated levels of dopamine, but many mind-altering substances artificially jack the fun juice. We become habituated to higher dopamine

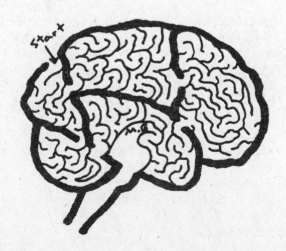

levels and/or the midbrain loses its ability to produce natural dopamine levels and voilà: We're addicted.

Dopamine disorder with roots in the midbrain also causes Parkinson's disease. We use the collection of dopamine neurons known as the direct pathway to move, and the indirect pathway tamps down unwanted movement. In Parkinson's disease, dopamine neurons in both pathways die. And so Parkinson's sufferers lose the direct pathway's ability to move voluntarily, while also losing the mellowing effects of the indirect pathway, resulting in involuntary movements such as shaking.

THE ECONOMICS OF MATING IV: GENDER SCARCITY

The models of human mating we've explored all assume an equal number of men and women. But what if this wasn't the case?

Think about Manhattan, where women outnumber men 10 to 9. In this shortness of male supply, men can drive a hard bargain: there are relatively few married Manhattan men in their twenties. Sure, you can point to high levels of education and a focus on career as reasons for this, but the plot thickens: A study of fashion from 1885 to 1976 found that in periods of male scarcity, hemlines rise. In other words, female competition equals short skirts.

But this male scarcity that leads to fewer married females also leads to increased female focus on career and empowerment. For example, look at the period of male scarcity during the Vietnam War. Scarce males drove loose sexual mores—can you say Woodstock and free love?—while unfettered women drove empowerment (OK, OK, there was the Pill too).

But what happens when women are scarce? We saw this in the early southern United States due to the agricultural economy. Amid female scarcity, cherished and protected Southern belles developed. Males were terrified of the potential for female philandering borne of unequal gender ratios. And increased male competition makes for especially warlike men. Luckily, duels, wars, and

Brains vs. Brawn

Throughout the animal kingdom, males that compete for females spend energy building brains and brawn (horns, claws, etc., and the mental ability to compete socially). But the males of free-love species compete too . . . via internal sperm competition. Winning the sperm battle requires, shall we say, *endowment resulting in volume.* Thus, depending on whether paternal competition is external or internal, a species develops brains or bollocks—very rarely both.

Where would you rank humans on this spectrum?

other testosterone-soaked competitions tend to lower a male majority back into balance with the female population.

Beware: In China, men currently outnumber women 6 to 5.

EYE HACK: THE WATERFALL ILLUSION

Look at a waterfall for thirty seconds. Now look at something stationary. The stationary object will appear to drift upward. The same phantom movement is true after stepping off an airport walkway: If you close your eyes and stand still, you should continue to feel yourself moving.

Though neither of these likely comes as a surprise, their cause is cool: When you first look at or experience a stimulus, the neurons that recognize it get excited. They spring into action, processing the new information and forcing it into your consciousness: *Wow, look at all that falling water!* Then the neurons get bored. The stimulus gets blasé and drifts into the background. And your neurons adjust their expected baseline—falling water starts to look stationary—and you start to interpret things in relation to this baseline. And if falling is stationary, then stationary is up, so when you look from a waterfall to a rock, your baseline is off and the rock appears to levitate until your neurons readjust.

But what's really cool is this: Looking at something moving (a waterfall) can make you *feel like you're moving* (the walkway). In other words, the phantom sensations cross. Maybe you've had the jolting sensation of moving backward as a large truck slowly passes your car on the freeway.

Researchers demonstrated this phenomenon by showing participants images of black and white bars moving up or down through a computer screen, and then touching participants' fingertips with a small electric device. Participants felt the device moving even if it wasn't.

But what's really, really cool is this: The effect crossed the other way too. A moving touch stimulus made participants feel as if a screen of black and white bars was moving, even if it wasn't.

CLOWNS' SELF-PURPOSE

A formal study of the psychology of clowns and comedians found that most felt it was their duty to make light of terrible situations, thus shielding humanity from the bad of the universe (though they said it a bit differently). Interestingly, this is exactly the role of the earliest court jesters, who were thought to magically intercede on a ruler's behalf against potentially malignant forces of all kinds. If the food taster was a shield against physical poison, the jester was a shield against psychological poison.

Psy-Op: Moving Walkway

Beware the moving walkway that isn't moving. Because you've been on moving walkways before, your body's learned to quickly and automatically adjust its baseline for the acceleration of stepping aboard. If you come across a stopped walkway—even if you consciously recognize that it's stopped—it's difficult to force your neurons *not* to adjust for the expected acceleration. And so you trip over your toes.

NAILS AND THE HUMAN BRAIN

• On January 6, 2005, twenty-three-year-old construction worker Patrick Lawler went to the dentist complaining of a toothache. After six days of eating ice cream to help the swelling, Lawler felt it was finally time to seek help. The dentist found a four-inch nail embedded in Lawler's brain, next to his right eye. Apparently, Lawler had fired a nail gun through a piece of rotten wood but didn't realize the nail had shot clean through the wood and

Not by Nails Alone

While nails are the brain-poking standby, they're not the only foreign bodies to be shot, shoved, or stabbed into the human brain. For example, after getting into a fistfight, a man reported to his local emergency room with a headache, black eye, and a cut on his cheek. Imaging found a 10.5-centimeter paintbrush embedded in the man's brain. Surgery removed the paintbrush and the man experienced no lasting effects. The paintbrush had entered bristles-first.

Or take the case of a man who drilled a hole in his head and then fed into he hole the uncoiled wire from a sketchpad. He recovered, too.

But holding the Guinness Record for "largest object removed from human skull" is Michael Hill, who, after answering the door at a friend's house, was stabbed with an eight-inch survival knife. With the knife embedded to the hilt in his brain, he walked down the street to another friend's house. The knife was removed four hours later. Hill recovered with slight memory loss and paralysis in his left hand.

then through the roof of his open mouth. Surgery removed the nail and Lawler recovered fully.

• In 2006, a thirty-three-year-old man in Portland, Oregon, went to the emergency room complaining of a headache. Doctors found twelve two-inch nails embedded in the man's head. The man had been high on methamphetamines and suicidal when he'd used a nail gun to fire the nails into his head the previous night. Doctors pulled the nails with needle-nosed pliers and a drill. The man recovered fully.

• In 2007, a man wearing a baseball cap complained of headaches at the emergency room of St. George's Hospital in London. Doctors removed the baseball cap to find eleven nails penetrating the man's brain, one of which was a spike at least five inches long. It turns out that the man had a history of paranoid schizophrenia and had hammered one nail into his head each of the previous eleven weeks in order to rid himself of evil. He recovered with no lasting neurological deficits.

• In 2008, when Kansas man George Chandler fired a nail deep into his brain, a resource-ful emergency room doctor removed the offending nail with a claw hammer.

• In 1993, a very drunk man was brought to his local emergency room. Even once he sobered up, he was seen to have weakness on the right side of his body (hemiparesis). The emergency room doctors ordered brain imaging. The images showed a two-inch nail, which had entered the patient's skull directly between his eyes and traveled through the brain to the very back of the skull. The man admitted to a suicide attempt nearly twelve years earlier.

We know the human brain is a device to keep the ears from grating on one another.

—Peter De Vries

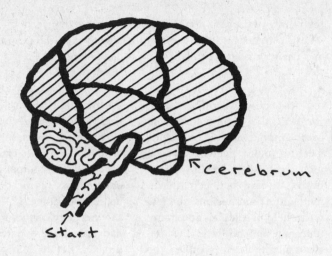

Cerebrum

Start

PIECE OF MIND: CEREBRUM

The cerebrum is an umbrella term encompassing the frontal, parietal, occipital, and temporal lobes. And fittingly, it looks much like an umbrella, cupped atop the brain stem and other goodies. It is this umbrella that makes humans human.

According to paleoneurologists, the first structure we'd call a brain emerged in reptiles about 500 million years ago. It was little more than a brain stem, capable of maintaining bodily functions, foraging for food, and mating (much like pubescent males). This "lizard brain" remains much unchanged in humans and other mammals; almost all advances have been in the area of the cerebrum.

Interestingly, in mammals, the size of the cerebrum and even the number of neurons it contains may have less to do with intelligence, emotion, and higher-order thinking than do its folds and the density of its connections. A folded cerebrum offers significantly more surface area for the organization of specialized processing centers. And adding a handful of neuronal connections increases the potential pathways of information through the brain much more so than adding a handful of neurons themselves.

JOCKS, NERDS, AND THE SECRETS OF SUCCESS

In 1926 and 1936, psychologist Catharine Cox published the results of studies she performed on 282 prominent leaders and thinkers. She hoped to discover what creates success.

As you'd expect, she found that both IQ and health were strong predictors of success. No surprise there.

But check this out: IQ and physical health are inversely related to each other. (Sickly people are smarter.) Why? Some think it's tied to sickly kids' habit of spending more time reading and studying. Others think humans have a finite amount of energy for use in development, and that some people prioritize brain and others brawn. But whatever the cause, it seems there's biological support for the stereotype of the smart nerd and dumb jock.

Wait a minute. Didn't Cox's study show that IQ and physical health have the *same* effect on success? Yep. This implies that nerds go through IQ to success, while jocks are able to skip that pesky IQ step on their way to the top echelons of society (remember, we're talking about averages of a large population here—your individual experience may vary).

More precisely, there are many kinds of "success" and while IQ and health are overall predictors, they're even stronger predictors of certain types of success. For example, great commanders score very high in physical health, while great writers score very low in physical health and very high in IQ.

BUT JOCKS GET BETTER GRADES

You might already know that attractive people are more likely than their plain rivals to be hired or to win elections. In psychology, this is referred to as a *beauty premium* and the flip side as a *plainness penalty* (cosmetic surgeons refer to the proven value of beauty as a *cash cow*).

Do these beauty premiums and plainness penalties extend to high school? Are the hotties and cool guys given better grades because of their beauty? While the cynic in you might be predisposed to say yes, the answer is actually no: Beauty doesn't help grades.

Actually, a better answer is *it's complex*.

Beauty does affect grades. Studied alone, prettier people receive higher grades. But when you take out personal grooming and personality, beauty predicts *lower* grades.

Huh? English please! OK:

People seen as beautiful are likely to possess both good grooming and strong personalities—but it's these and not beauty itself that result in higher high school grades. In fact, in a population of students who have it all—good grooming and strong personalities—the students who are also especially beautiful will earn (or be given) lower grades. So the true predictors of high grades are grooming and personality. And listen up, you gross boys and mean girls: For boys, grooming is more important, and for girls, it's personality.

If high-schoolers get nice and get clean, they can combat the beauty premium.

ATKINS MAKES YOU DUMB?

Our brain eats glucose. And it needs a steady stream because our brain's nerve cells burn glucose like spark plugs burn drops of gas. Because we can't store glucose as itself and because it's unrealistic to eat exactly one piece of candy corn every 23.8 seconds, we throw bigger logs on the fire and trust our bodies to chip away at these logs, breaking them down into the steady stream of glucose our brain needs.

These logs are carbohydrates. Take away carbohydrates and you commit to a boom and bust cycle of brain food. At least that's what a Tufts University study found. Researchers studied dieters, with half the dieters

Mental power cannot be got from ill-fed brains.

—Herbert Spencer

cutting calories and half cutting carbohydrates. The low-carb dieters underperformed the low-calorie dieters on memory tasks. Researchers blamed the difference on lack of carbs leading to lack of glucose.

Apparently no pay equals no play in the brain.

LOGIC OF ILLOGIC: BRAIN-DEFLATING FALLACIES TO WIN ANY ARGUMENT, PART III

Still more strategies to ensure dominance in debate club and/or with an unsuspecting significant other:

• False dilemma: There may be other options. . . . *"Either you admit that you ate the ice cream, or you admit once and for all that you've been spiriting away jamocha almond fudge to a secret freezer in the basement."*

• Golden mean fallacy: The truth is found in compromise. *"OK, OK, let's just admit that we're both wrong."*

• Mistaking logic for truth: The argument is logical, only the premises might not be. *"If I bogarted the very last of the jamocha almond fudge, I would have at least one almond stuck in my teeth. I have no such almond(s). Thus am I exonerated!"*

• Naturalistic fallacy: Making a moral judgment based on a statement of fact only. *"I bought the ice cream in the first place. Thus, it's only right that I eat the last of it."*

• Nomical fallacy: Naming is explaining. *"You see, I'm thermophobic and thus must seek sugary, icy-cold desserts."*

GENIUS TESTER #4: BOXES OF BARS

You have ten boxes of one-pound gold bars, one of which contains counterfeits with bars weighing one-twentieth of a pound less than real bars. With only one weighing, how can you determine the counterfeit box?

Eye Hack: Gray Square Illusion

Our brain is especially adept at interpreting the effects of lighting. We interpret this picture as a cylinder casting a shadow on a chessboard. And so square B should be lighter than square A, only, it's in the shadow. Actually, the two squares are exactly the same shade.

EYE HACK: CHENEY-MONSTER

One is an upside-down picture of Dick Cheney. The other is a horrible monster. Turn the images upright to see which is which.

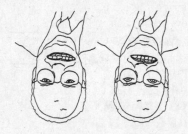

CORTICAL HOMUNCULUS

Your brain's sensory neurons are plastered across your primary motor cortex like stars in a planetarium. When the stars twinkle, you feel pressure or pain. And every sensory neuron has a corresponding sensory nerve in your fingertip, left knee, shoulder, or elsewhere. But while sensory nerves are packed tightly in your fingertips and spread widely in the middle of your back, the corresponding sensory neurons are spread evenly in the primary motor cortex.

This means that your brain's representation of your body proportions is very different from the proportions of your body itself. This brain representation is your cortical homunculus: he has big hands, big lips, a big tongue, and a big . . . well, you know. Don't be embarrassed—everybody has one.

In addition to his mismatched proportions, your homunculus is strangely arranged. For example, the sensory neurons that accept signals from your left hand are just next to those that recognize feelings in your left cheek. If the sensory neurons of the left hand die or stop firing, the sensory neurons from the left cheek grow into the vacated space.

This means that a touch to the cheek of a one-handed person may feel as if it's also touching the missing hand.

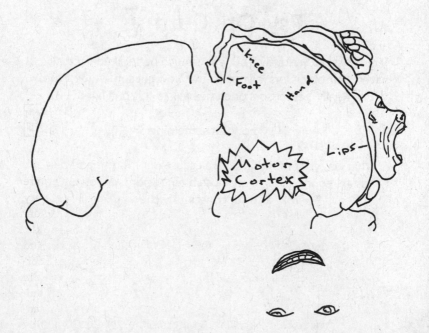

Psy-Op: Cutting

Find scissors. Seriously. This works much better if you actually have a pair of scissors in your hands. Now cut something. Stop! Really, get scissors or come back to this one later.

OK, now cut something.

What was your mouth doing? Because our mouths and our hands are controlled by very close brain regions, as you cut you may also subconsciously chew.

EXPECTED VALUE, EXPECTED UTILITY, AND PROSPECT THEORY

How do we make decisions? Well, when a decision has obvious results, we make the choice that returns the best result. Duh. This is like looking at a buffet set with many different foods: if you want the lobster, just walk over and choose lobster.

But what about the many, many times you're forced to make a choice without knowing its outcome? Or a choice based on incomplete information? Maybe the foods are covered and only one platter holds the lobster. Maybe you wonder if the buffet's price is worth the uncertain payoff.

This is a gamble.

One way to decide if a gamble's worthwhile is to evaluate its *expected value*. Imagine there are 38 platters. On one platter is lobster. The others are empty. Not a very good gamble, eh? But check this out: It costs only a buck to pick a platter and the lobster's worth $35. Is it a good gamble now? Well, 1 time out of 38, you win a $35 lobster, and 37 times out of 38, you lose your dollar bet.

Here's the expected value (remember the term *expected value!* But feel free to skip the math if you want):

$$\left(\frac{1}{38} \times \$35\right) - \left(\frac{37}{38} \times \$1\right) = -\$0.0526$$

If you haven't already guessed, this is roulette. While it's true that you might oscillate between being up and being down, over time you can expect the wheel to take just over five cents of your dollar.

But what are the winnings— say a $35 lobster—*really worth*? Are you a connoisseur? Does lobster make you recall memories of your childhood in Maine? Are you allergic to shellfish? Are you trying to impress a date? The key point here is that while the bug may have a $35 price tag, its "utility" is different for different people. To you, it might be worth $100 or it might be worth nothing.

And look: In our 1-in-38 bet with a $35 payout, it takes only one dollar of increased utility to make the bet break even. So what's the payout's utility to you? Think of roulette again; what *else* do you get from playing? Free drinks? Excitement? Power? A coronary? Increased likelihood of romantic attention? Sweaty armpits? And what does the dollar lost mean to you? Are you a Rockefeller or a raga-muffin? Is losing the bet a fair price to pay for the experience? Look at the equation. Adjust the "prices" accordingly. Now, does the expected utility of the bet make it worthwhile?

Let's switch from roulette to poker: Imagine a tournament. If you're looking at two identical hands—the same cards with the same bets on the table—at different points in the tournament, the *expected value* of your own bet stays constant: One situation's exactly the same as the next and you should bet the situations equally.

But while expected value stays the same, your bet's *expected utility* might change: In the early stages of a tournament, your goal is to stick around (until others bust and the remaining players get paid), but later, your goal is to amass a big stack of chips as quickly as possible. And so in the early stages of a poker tournament, you're *risk averse,* and in the later stages, you're *risk neutral* or even *risk accepting.* (Again, expected value of a hand doesn't change, but its expected utility does.) This means that faced with the tricky choice to call or fold early in the tournament, you might fold; faced with the same choice later, you might call.

So, making decisions based on expected value (cold, hard numbers) and then adjusting them for our own expected utility (adding logical "soft" factors) is what we *should* do whenever faced with this kind of decision. But what do we *actually* do?

To some degree we follow these rules: Our brain automatically computes expected utility and then picks the choice with the highest utility. Only, we don't do it very well. Our logic can be led. Based on factors as seemingly inconsequential as the temperature of the drink we're holding, we judge utility differently. This expected utility plus human illogic is called prospect theory, and it won its creators a Nobel Prize.

Luckily, somewhere deep within the folds of our brain, we *know* we're bad at computing utility. And so we play life as if it were the opening rounds of a poker tournament: we're risk averse. All else equal, we play it safe: The pain of losing a dollar is greater than the joy of winning a dollar.

But good thing for state lotteries, the pain of losing a dollar is worth the excitement of potentially winning a million dollars, even when it's a very, very bad bet! Thank you, prospect theory. . . .

Risk Aversion in Action

Would you risk $5 for the 50/50 chance to win $10? What if the payoff was $12? If you still say no, you're risk averse. But who cares about five bucks? To see how humans behave when the stakes are high, Dutch researchers turned to game shows, specifically *Deal Or No Deal*, a game with little strategy and defined odds. Their results? First, contestants are broadly risk averse, willing to risk small sums for only potential payoffs 1.61 times greater than expected value (risking $10 on a coin toss to win $32), and large sums for payoffs 2.15 times greater (risking $10 on a coin toss to win $43). Second, the shape of the game affects players' behavior—a big loss leads to risk seeking as players try to "break even." And finally, how contestants frame events affects their behavior—contestants "going on gut" are very risk averse, contestants looking toward the next bank offer are somewhat less so, and contestants concerned primarily with how results affect the likely amount in their final case are only slightly risk averse.

LOGIC OF ILLOGIC: LUXURY BLOODLUST

You want that $145,000 car, don't you. You want it *real bad.* Or that $275 bottle of wine. And we want these things more than if the same items were priced at $24,000 and $7.99 respectively. But this flies in the face of basic economics: Traditionally, lower prices create *more* demand, not less (this is why all the sale bread is gone by the time you get to the grocery store after work).

*The mind is its own place,
and in itself
Can make a Heaven of Hell,
a Hell of Heaven.*

—John Milton, *Paradise Lost*

Good thing for Lotus and Château Margaux we're susceptible to the Veblen effect: *We want more expensive products because these products imply status.*

But is this so irrational? Are some things actually worth paying more for when we could pay less?

Researchers at Stanford explored our feelings about $5 and $45 wine. Only they changed the price tag on exactly the same bottle. As you might expect, people expected and thus found more quality in the $45 bottle.

But here's the thing: It wasn't just people being snooty. To the brain, these were different wines. This is true to the point of increased activity in the brain's pleasure center (medial orbitofrontal cortex) while tasting the higher-priced bottle. Again: A higher price actually makes people *experience* a different wine.

And how we perceive an item increases not only our opinion of it, but also its effectiveness. For example, people who paid full price for Red Bull and expected the drink to increase their attention were able to solve more brainteasers than people who paid less for the same drink. (Similar is true of painkillers.)

GAME THEORY MAKE BRAIN BIG: KUHN POKER

Two players share a three-card deck: Jack, Queen, and King. The highest card wins. You each ante one chip. You each get a card. The third card remains unseen. The first player can check or bet one chip. Player two can call, fold, check, or raise one. If needed, player one can then call or fold (no reraising).

Obviously, if you're confronted by a bet, there's no reason to call with a Jack and no reason to fold with a King. But what do you do if you're holding a Queen and playing first?

AUTHORITY AND THE STRIP-SEARCH PRANK CALL

Do you remember Stanley Milgram's famous authority experiments, which found participants were willing to shock the living hell out of people if ordered to do so? (If not, Google "Milgram experiment" and get ready for some scary reading.)

In an environment much less controlled than Milgram's' lab at Yale, a researcher of a different sort found similar results. From 1995 to 2004, a prankster pretending to be a police officer called fast food chains and ordered store managers to strip-search their employees. And commonly, managers obeyed.

At least seventy calls were reported.

The prankster's more creative successes include convincing a female McDonald's manager to undress in front of customers, one of whom the prankster identified as a suspected sex offender. The manager believed she was acting as bait and that when the purported sex offender moved in to attack, undercover police would swoop in to arrest him.

AH, THE TEENAGE (Y)EARS

Kids love sneaky spy technology. OK, guys continue to love sneaky spy technology. But kids have one very specific advantage: As we age, we lose the top end of our hearing. Generally, kids can hear pitches up to 17 kilohertz, while adults are limited by the ear decay known as presbycusis to 15 kilohertz or less (for comparison, the highest note on a piano is 4 kilohertz).

Here's the spy gadgetry angle: Originally, the device known as the *Mosquito* was meant to clear loitering teens from street corners by loudly broadcasting an annoying pitch only the young loiterers could hear. But sneaky, sneaky teens co-opted the device for their own dark-hat purposes: a ring tone audible to only teen ears. Imagine it: text message alerts during class, secret signals via cell, the eventual return to the fluid use of Morse code.

The ring tone, called Teen Buzz, can be downloaded everywhere. The *New York Times* piece describing this sneaky audio table-turning calls it techno-jujitsu. The balance of power has shifted.

LOGIC OF ILLOGIC: YOU CAN'T MAKE ME EAT PIE

Female undergrads were asked to rate the taste of three Argentinean desserts. In the course of many tasting sessions, half the girls were allowed to choose from the three, while the other girls were assigned to taste only the dessert that the other group had given the highest rating.

Then all girls were assigned pie. How do you think the two groups rated the pie?

The group assigned desserts throughout liked the pie just fine, while the group who'd been choosing, like, totally dissed the assigned dessert (as if!).

While illogical to most, this will come as no surprise to parents of teenage girls: Taking away freedom provokes backlash. Forbidding dessert choice in girls

iDread

Ephebiphobia: fear of teenagers.

who were used to choosing desserts for themselves meant that anything put in front of them—no matter how scrumptious—was doomed to disgust. (Talk to the hand, pie!)

Medical patients do the same thing. When freedoms are restricted, they may disobey treatment recommendations. Both parents of teenage girls and doctors of uncooperative patients can increase compliance by increasing daughter/patient control over the situation and by increasing their own credibility.

Eye Hack: Penrose Stairs

Your likelihood of walking to the top of these stairs equals your chance of pacifying the average teenage girl. The Penrose stairs work by distorting perspective, especially in the back-left slope, in which stairs rise but the overall slope must lower. Check online for an audio clip called a Shepherd Tone, which seems to continually lower without ever actually going anywhere.

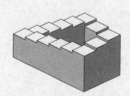

YOUR PERSONALIZED HOROSCOPE

Based on the very specific personality type that would buy this book and read this far into it, here is a personally tailored horoscope:

You have a need for other people to like and admire you, and yet you tend to be critical of yourself. While you have some personality weaknesses, you are generally able to compensate for them. You have considerable unused capacity that you have not turned to your advantage. Disciplined and self-controlled on the outside, you tend to be worrisome and insecure on the inside. At times you have serious doubts as to whether you have made the right decision or done the right thing. You prefer a certain amount of change and variety and become dissatisfied when hemmed in by restrictions and limitations. You also pride yourself as an independent thinker and do not accept others' statements without satisfactory proof. But you have found it unwise to be too frank in revealing yourself to others. At times you are extroverted, affable, and sociable, while at other times you are introverted, wary, and reserved. Some of your aspirations tend to be rather unrealistic.

Spooky, huh? On a scale of one to five (five high), how accurate do you consider this horoscope? Isn't it amazing how precisely the books you read describe who you are?

In 1948, psychologist Bertram R. Forer did a similar experiment with his UCLA students, having them take personality tests and then offering personalized horoscopes based on the tests' very specific results. When he asked students to rate the horoscopes' accuracy, students gave them an average of 4.26 out of five. Only, he gave all his students exactly the same horoscope . . . which was exactly the same as the one you just read above.

This experiment is a favorite of psych 101 classes and tends to return results very similar to Forer's original numbers.

E-PERSONALITY

Check out these e-mail addresses: honney.bunny77@hotmail.com, jane.doe@nasa.gov, rad dude69@mobileme.com, Cmndr Spud@6zap.com. Now, who's the tech geek, who's the professional, who's the cheerleader, and who's the poseur guy? A German study confirmed what you already know: We can infer a sender's personality from his or her e-mail address. In the study, a 100-person panel was asked to guess the personalities of 600 people, based on only e-mail addresses. Then researchers compared these guesses with the e-mail owners' responses on a personality quiz. E-mail addresses significantly outed participants' neuroticism, openness, agreeableness, conscientiousness, and narcissism, but failed to predict their extraversion. Especially telling were addresses that used numbers, periods, and names other than the sender's own.

The juvenile sea squirt wanders through the sea searching for a suitable rock or hunk of coral to cling to and make its home for life. For this task, it has a rudimentary nervous system. When it finds its spot and takes root, it doesn't need its brain anymore, so it eats it! (It's rather like getting tenure.)

—Daniel C. Dennett,
Consciousness Explained

Eye Hack: Oscillating Face

Be assured, this is a simple, two-dimensional image, conventionally printed. But our mind allows a very limited range of possibilities for the human face, and so repeatedly tells the eyes they must have made a mistake. And you continue to tick and tock back and forth between the "real" interpretation.

SELF-TEST: PERSONALITY SNAPSHOT

How closely do the following phrases describe you? Use a pencil to score each question from 1 to 5 with 1 being "very inaccurate" and 5 being "very accurate." Then check the back of the book for interpretation.

1. Am the life of the party.

2. Sympathize with others' feelings.

3. Get chores done right away.

4. Have frequent mood swings.

5. Have a vivid imagination.

6. Don't talk a lot.

7. Am not interested in other people's problems.

8. Often forget to put things back in their proper place.

9. Am relaxed most of the time.

10. Am not interested in abstract ideas.

11. Talk to a lot of different people at parties.

12. Feel others' emotions.

13. Like order.

14. Get upset easily.

15. Understand abstract ideas.

16. Keep in the background.

17. Am not really interested in others.

18. Make a mess of things.

19. Seldom feel blue.

20. Do not have a good imagination.

FUZZY LOGIC

No one speaks exactly like you do. Sure, your parents and siblings are close (except your brother Pete, who still calls the morning meal "breakferest"), but the words that enter your ears are never exactly those that come out your mouth. Still, you generally know what people are saying when they wag their pie holes.

This is because your mind is fuzzy.

We don't need to hear language that *precisely* matches our expectations. We only need sounds that make our brains' interpretations *very likely.* This is fuzzy logic: making judgments that aren't simply true or false, but are somewhere on the spectrum between the two. Thus when Pete says "breakferest" you know he's *most likely* referring to the morning meal.

And your brain does this all the time. Is a room hot or cold? Is that a good pitch to swing at? Is a person short or tall? Are you tired or energized? Are you fashionably or rudely late? Are you sufficiently caffeinated? When is a fellow freeway driver a threat? None of these is an either/or choice—we evaluate them all on gradients—and where they are on these sliding scales affects our behavior. Maybe when a slider hits a certain tipping point, you take an afternoon nap, or swing for the fence, or give that chip-eating, cell-talking, radio-fiddling driver a little extra space.

In addition to creating our basic ability to communicate with other human beings and exist in a messy world, fuzzy logic is useful when cooking rice. To most rice cookers, rice is simply "cooked" or "not." If "not," the machine keeps cooking. If "cooked," it stops. Not so with the Zojirushi NS-ZCC10. Like the human mind, the machine senses gradients—*mostly raw, partially cooked, almost there, shit it's burning,* etc.—and adjusts its behavior based on these partial states. For example, a fuzzy logic cooker may sense its rice cooking too quickly on a hot day and turn the heat slightly lower.

And rice cookers aren't the only application of fuzzy logic outside the brain. Think about your photo-retouching software that's able to find where a person stops and the background starts. Finding this edge isn't an all-or-nothing proposition. It's fuzzy. You go from "definitely person" to "definitely background" but between the two, the software uses fuzzy logic to pick where to

Fzzuy Rdaeing

The barin's fzzuy ligoc alowls you to raed tihs, deipste the jumlbed lteetr odrer. It wuold be mcuh hdraer if the fisrt or lsat ltteers wree mvoed.

draw the actual line. Your e-mail spam filter uses fuzzy logic too: What's the percentage chance that an e-mail containing the words *refinance, national lottery,* and *pen1s* is spam?

Fuzzy logic also makes *The Lord of the Rings; WALL-E, I, Robot; Eragon; Flags of Our Fathers;* and many other movies possible. Each of these movies contains a massive crowd or battle scene. And in each of these scenes, the fuzzy logic of a simulation software called Massive digitally controls the movements of the people within these crowds. Imagine a human crowd: Each person acts independently, using group cues to guide their own movements. Thus sections of the crowd stop and start at different speeds, edges morph in different directions, and individuals sometimes veer from the group's exact direction. But the whole creates the effect of a fairly homogenous moving blob. The same is true with Massive—each individual is pushed, pulled, and bounced by others in the group, but the overall crowd moves like a crowd.

Are you too tired to keep reading? Maybe you have time for just one more topic?

It's fuzzy.

Fuzzy History

Blame fuzzy logic on Plato, who first posited that between true and false is a region where things are both partly true and partly false.

ASCH CONFORMITY EXPERIMENTS

Take a look at the leftmost bar. Does its length match line A, B, or C on the right card? It doesn't take a neurosurgeon to see that it matches line C. In fact, only one in thirty-five people get this question wrong when asked individually.

But 36.8 percent of Solomon Asch's test subjects answered the question incorrectly.

Why? They were duped by da group: Alongside ringers who were instructed to pick line A or B, test subjects switched their opinions to match those of the group.

Variations of the experiment found that it takes three or more people voicing a unanimous opinion to make a subject go along with an obviously incorrect choice. And if even one other member in a large group dissents, it frees the subject to dissent too, even if the first dissenter expresses an incorrect opinion.

Genius Tester #5: Mr. Smith's Children

In 1959, science writer Martin Gardner published the following puzzle in *Scientific American*:

- Mr. Jones has two children, the eldest of whom is a girl. What's the probability that both children are girls?

- Mr. Smith has two children, at least one of whom is a boy. What's the probability that both children are boys?

Check the solution. It's as good as the puzzle.

WILD KINGDOM: GUPPY GAMES

When pondering conformity in the animal kingdom, your first question probably is *what about the Trinidadian Turure River guppies?* Yes, in fact these guppies have highly developed strategies that ensure that any nail sticking up is hammered down.

Specifically, they play the game theory strategy Tit-for-Tat (see Be Nice, but Not Too Nice: Game Theory Says So). When a sunfish or other predator approaches a guppy school, it's in the group's best interest to assess the threat—is the sunfish hungry? And so a squadron of guppy scouts approaches the predator. Guppies in the scouting party have two options: They can advance (unsafe) or they can refuse (safe).

Here's what they do: On the first "move" a guppy will advance toward the threat. And then it's another guppy's turn to take the lead. As long as the others in the party advance, so too will intrepid scout #1. And so after the scouting party is initiated, guppies mimic one another's advance/refuse patterns. This is Tit-for-Tat.

But the game has a twist. If a guppy proves especially unwilling to take its turn, the other guppies in the scouting party may reposition themselves behind the reluctant fish, thus forcing wussy-fish to pay an evolutionary price for his cowardice.

This system ensures that it's in an individual guppy's best interest to act in the group's best interest.

Think about this in terms of human vaccinations. Every kid who gets poked runs a slight risk of ill effects (this risk now outweighs the risk of getting the disease itself). But it's in the interest of the group that everyone is vaccinated. Without other incentives, game theory predicts that humans would act in their individual best interests and refuse vaccines. This is why we have the equivalent of guppy enforcers: PTAs, play groups, and peewee soccer parents whose job it is to excommunicate those who refuse vaccinations, just like the guppies pushing Cowardly Joe to the front lines of sunfish inspection.

Psy-Op: No Soap Radio

Joke: A penguin and a polar bear are sitting in a bathtub. The penguin says, "Please pass the soap." The polar bear says, "No soap . . . radio!"

When you tell this joke in a group, everyone explodes in laughter. That's because you've told everyone but one person to fake it. As you might've noticed, the joke itself is completely unfunny. What *is* funny is the one person who almost inevitably laughs along with the group, pretending to get it.

their guess as to what two-thirds of the average guess will be. (If the average of all guesses was 60 and you guessed 40, you'd win.)

What's your most logical guess? Assume that everyone guessing has mastered the mental zen of game theory.

Each person in a group picks a number from 0 to 100. But here's how they pick: Their number is

Debunked:
The Happy Herd

Many fish flashing as a coordinated school is a beautiful example of group cooperation against predators. Right?

Evolutionary biologist W. D. Hamilton offered another explanation: The fish that most successfully mimics the movements of those around it never pops out the center of the school. And the center is the safest. So a fish school's coordination is due to many individuals working in their own self-interest, rather than to any groovy melding of fishy minds for the common good.

Get Over It:
The End of Shame

Shame has a distinct evolutionary purpose: You've acted against social norms and thus rent the very fabric of society on which human civilization depends (not to be overly dramatic or anything), and it's shame that brings you back in line.

When shame reaches a certain level, you internalize it, start to consider yourself a bad apple, and can effectively prune your malignant self from the social tree ("I can never show my face in that bar ever again!"). This can be debilitating. More adaptive is to turn outward and sally forth into society to repair the rip you created. Only by repairing social connections— by apologizing or otherwise making amends—can you truly root out shame.

Genius Tester #6: Four Squares Problem

Reposition two and only two sticks to make four squares of equal size, with no sticks left over.

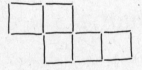

Courtesy of John DiPrete at www.mindbluff.com.

Want to be happy? Researchers at the Mayo Clinic know how. Unfortunately, some of the most important factors in creating happiness are out of your control: Women are happier than men, genetics matter, and the midlife crisis is real with happiness peaks in the young and old (or does happiness help people live longer, skewing the results?).

But one major factor *is* in your hands. Simply engaging in activities of your choosing, especially if you're mindful of this choice, can boost happiness significantly.

The Mayo study found this effect to be especially powerful in the context of goals. For example, fame, beauty, and other

Beauty can't amuse you, but brainwork— reading, writing, thinking—can.

—Helen Gurley Brown

goals that require external recognition are good in the chasing (any goal adds purpose), but not so good in the having.

Interestingly, the study found that as long as basic needs are met, wealth has no effect on happiness.

SELF-TEST

Read the following statements and use a pencil to score each question's accuracy in describing your thoughts or behaviors, with one being "very inaccurate" and five being "very accurate." Flip to the back of the book for interpretation.

1. I feel threatened easily.

2. I am sure of my ground.

3. I adapt easily to new situations.

4. I often feel blue.

5. I worry about things.

6. I feel comfortable with myself.

7. I am filled with doubts about things.

8. I look at the bright side of life.

9. I dislike myself.

10. I seldom feel blue.

Twins and Sex

OK, hold your horses. It's not like that. But it's still pretty good: A King's College London study of more than 2,000 female twins found that the twin with higher emotional intelligence had more orgasms. It's that simple: Females who are in touch with their emotions have more orgasms than those who are out of touch.

Wow.

LOGIC OF ILLOGIC: BRAIN-DEFLATING FALLACIES TO WIN ANY ARGUMENT, PART IV

Still more strategies to ensure dominance in debate club and/or with an unsuspecting significant other:

• Post hoc, ergo propter hoc: Because x follows y, y *caused* x. *"See? Now you have an upset stomach! Thus, my dear wife, you and not I have eaten the last of the jamocha almond fudge!"*

• Red herring: An unrelated fact throws off the scent. *"You will, of course, have noticed that even now every piece of pickled herring remains firmly jarred!"*

• Slippery slope: A supposed string of causes and effects, with a massively undesirable endpoint. *"Honey, if you keep fixating on the fate of the jamocha almond fudge, you won't be able to sleep and you'll lie awake all night wondering if maybe you're the one who ate the ice cream, and then you'll start questioning reality in general, and before you know it, you'll be pulling your hair and muttering gibberish down by the waterfront."*

• Straw man: Mischaracterizing an opinion to the point of parody. *"So you're saying that I'm incapable of love and was likely the second shooter on the grassy knoll?"*

• You too: Distracting from fault by counterattack. *"Yeah, but last week you drank the last Redhook Double Black Stout!* Seriously, have you no speck of human decency?"*

---

* Cases of above beverage can be sent to this author care of Three Rivers Press.

EYE HACK: WHICH OF THESE FACES IS HAPPIER?

The only (major) difference between these faces is the mouth tilt. Because input from the left eye crosses to the brain's right hemisphere—the area of the brain that processes expressions—we assign more importance to the left side of these images' mouths. Thus, the vast majority of people say the second image, with uplifted left side, is happier.

Zen Mind

Sozan was asked by a student: "What is the most valuable thing in the world?"

The master replied: "The head of a dead cat."

"Why is the head of a dead cat the most valuable thing in the world?" inquired the student.

Sozan replied: "Because no one can name its price."

iDread

Asymmetriphobia: fear of asymmetrical things.

Clasp your hands, interlocking your fingers. This feels natural. Now look at which pinky is on the bottom. Try clasping your hands with the other pinky down. It feels weird, right? Kind of like throwing a baseball with your off hand.

And for that, you can thank your parents. That's because the way you clasp your hands is largely determined by genetics (and independent of whether you're right- or left-handed).

When you cross your legs, which leg goes on top? Sixty-two percent cross the right leg over, and that's genetic too. The same genetic link is true of arm crossing.

You may already know that the ability to roll your tongue or move your ears is genetic. So is perfect pitch—the ability to recognize a note plunked on the piano without context. Stuttering is genetic too, as is the desire to seek novel experiences.

MEMORY I: ALTERNATE REALITIES

When we store events in our memories, we tag them with keywords. Was the roller-coaster ride exciting, or scary? Was the dip in the pool cold, or invigorating? Then when we encounter a similar situation, we run a quick keyword search of our memory to help us interpret the new event. Whether you go on the roller coaster or jump in the pool depends on how you tagged these experiences last time.

This gets more interesting when you consider that we all use different keywords. These keyword tags become part of our reality, and thus our "realities" differ.

Elizabeth Loftus and John Palmer showed this by forcing their own keyword tags onto subjects' memories. They had subjects watch video of a car crash and then asked them to estimate the cars' speeds. But the sneaky experimenters phrased the question five slightly different ways: 1. About how fast were the cars going when they hit each other? 2. About how fast were the cars going when they smashed each other? 3. About how fast were the cars going when they col-lided with each other? 4. About how fast were the cars going when they bumped into each other? 5. About how fast were the cars going when they contacted with each other?"

And so they tagged subjects' memories with the keywords "hit," "smashed," "collided," "bumped," and "contacted". Subjects' estimates when tagged with "smashed" averaged 9 mph faster than their estimates when tagged with "contacted."

Even spookier, though, is that this tagging didn't just affect people's *estimates* about the crash; it seemed to change their *memories* of the event as well. A week later when Loftus and Palmer asked subjects if the crash had produced broken glass, those whose memories were tagged with "smashed" said yes more often than those whose memories had been tagged with "contacted." For, of course, a *smash* breaks glass while a *contact* doesn't.

Gender Memory Smackdown

Loftus also looked into how the male and female memories differ. She found little difference in the amount of data men and women are able to remember. But (as you'd expect) she found very significant differences in *what* we remember. Male spatial memory is better and women are better at remembering faces and at tasks requiring verbal memory. Period.

Interestingly, the details that men and women best remember match stereotype. Eyewitness memory studies show that men remember the type of car, while women remember attributes of the driver. This stereotyping extends further: Men better remember "male-oriented" items (the gun), while women remember "female-oriented" items (the dress).

Loftus recommends "considerable caution" when attempting to explain these gender differences—do we blame biology or culture? In addition to (or instead of?) a physiological component, Loftus suggests that we remember what we most notice and that this is partly determined by what we're expected to notice—boys grew up playing gun games—and so at least in part, stereotype creates culture and culture creates gender-specific memory.

LOGIC OF ILLOGIC: SO GOD-AWFULLY BORING

Here's a peg. Screw it in this hole a quarter turn. Repeat. Again. Repeat. For an hour. As intended, this task is boring. Really, mind-numbingly boring. And after an hour any sane person has learned to hate it. But what if after spending an hour doing this, you were paid $20 to convince the next subject that the task is actually pretty fun? What if you were paid only $1 to sucker the next guy in?

How does the amount of money you were paid affect your feelings about the task itself? You probably remember the task a little more fondly if you got twenty bucks for it, right?

Nope.

Being paid $20 allows you to blame your behavior (convincing someone the task is fun) on the money, whereas if you earn only a buck, you have to otherwise justify your behavior—you convince yourself, at least in part, that turning pegs for an hour is fun. In other words, being paid allows you to say "that sucked but at least I got paid," while without money, you have to tell

yourself "I guess it really wasn't that bad."

And what you tell yourself becomes your belief.

MEMORY II: CREATING FALSE MEMORIES

We saw that Elizabeth Loftus is able to Jedi mind trick our interpretations of memories, but what about creating entirely new memories?

Oh yeah, baby. Actually, making a false memory is pretty easy. Loftus describes a father convincing his daughter she'd gotten lost in a mall when she was five years old. At first, the daughter denies any memory of the event, but as the father provides more fake details—"Don't you remember that I told you we would meet at the Tug Boat?"— the daughter begins to "remember" and even provide details of her own. Eventually when her father says "I was so scared," the daughter responds "Not as scared as I was!"

Loftus also showed subjects a painting of a country scene and then asked them to remember it:

the trees, the waving grain, the barn. Only, there was no barn in the image. Even though subjects knew there was no barn when they looked at the painting, those in whose heads the idea was planted recalled a barn when asked about it a couple weeks later.

You can probably imagine the implications of false memory in the courtroom or on the therapist's couch (which famously leads to the courtroom). But imagine the power of keyword tagging and false memory in advertising: How do you remember that box of cereal sitting on the grocery shelf?

MEMORY III: THE BRAIN-WORKS OF BAD MEMORY

OK, our memories are malleable. We can easily be made to misremember, and easily be made to adopt memories of things that never happened. But what actually goes on in our brains as we code bad information? Can we see misinformation taking hold?

Researchers Yoko Okado and Craig Stark can.

They showed subjects slides (correct information), and then showed them another set of slides with details changed (incorrect information). And they watched as subjects' hippocampi coded memories for both sets. Sure enough, the set of slides that most brightly lit subjects' hippocampi is the set subjects remembered—whether correct or incorrect.

Next, Okado and Stark monitored the prefrontal cortex, which remembers the sources of our memories. If the PFC's source tag was stronger for the fist set of slides, subjects thought that whatever they remembered had been shown in this first set. If the PFC lit brighter for the second set, subjects thought their information came from the second set.

Thus is a false memory born: The hippocampus remembers the wrong information and the prefrontal cortex believes it's from the original scene.

HERE TODAY, GONE IN MILLISECONDS: ICONIC MEMORY

What's shorter than short-term memory? The answer is *iconic memory*, the very accurate but very short-lived visual impression of something. Here's the thing about iconic memory: It's so fleeting that it's difficult even to detect—by the time you could verbally report something stored in only iconic memory, it's gone. So to test iconic memory, psychologist George Sperling came up with a tricky experiment: He asked participants to look very briefly at a grid of letters. Short-term memory should have allowed them to report four to six characters and, in fact, this is what Sperling found. But it turned out that immediately after glimpsing the grid, participants could reproduce *any* four-to-six character section of the grid—yes, their recall was restricted by the limits of short-term memory, but their iconic memory briefly held the whole thing in their minds.

(By the way, can you find the one common word in this entry's heading doodle?)

POST-STEREOTYPE

It's easy to imagine that an employer might judge an applicant's appearance and then see the traits he/she expects from this appearance. For example, because you have long hair, the interviewer finds you creative and individualistic (whereas if you'd gotten a close snip before the interview, the same person would find you detail-oriented and conscientious). This is stereotyping—we tend to make judgments about an individual based on a person's group. As you've probably heard, this is true to the point that an ethnic name can influence an employer's evaluation of an applicant's résumé.

But imagine this employer learns the information needed to stereotype (race, appearance, etc.) only *after* making individualized judgments—perhaps only after reading John Doe's résumé and exploring John's LinkedIn profile does the employer learn in an interview that John has long hair.

A 2009 study found hope for the human race in that our stereotypes are rarely able to change the judgments we make based on fact—as long as we make these fact-based judgments before getting the information needed to stereotype someone. In other words, finding out a candidate's race rarely changes the opinion an employer first created based on his or her résumé. But check this out: When stereotypes then *confirm* these fact-based judgments (i.e., when the stereotypes of a candidate's race *support* an employer's opinion of his résumé), they combine to create a nearly unbreakable evaluation.

It's as if a college football coach said, "I liked the look of that 14–0 record at Oaks Christian, and now that I know he's Joe Montana's son, he must be good!" (Author anxiously awaiting the future of Washington Huskies football.)

RACIAL BIAS IN STANDARDIZED TESTING?

Every fall, millions of American high school students take the SAT. And every year, the results of these tests show that non-Asian minorities underperform Caucasian students and that female students underperform male peers in quantitative fields. Traditionally, psychologists attribute these scores to real differences in ability caused by poverty, gender roles, etc.

But there may be another cause: black or female test takers' fears that performing poorly will reinforce others' negative stereotypes about them. This pressure creates lower scores.

Researchers at Stanford showed this by giving black and white sophomores a version of

All Work and No Play Makes Jack's Brain Dull

Do you work more than forty hours a week? If so, your brain's at risk. A study of 2,214 British civil servants found that work in excess of forty hours is associated with worse short-term memory and word recall.

the GRE test. In one group, subjects were told the test was simply a data-gathering tool; another group was told the test measured verbal and reasoning ability.

With the potential for stereotype in place—i.e., when test takers thought they were measuring verbal and reasoning ability—the black students scored lower than the other group.

What does this mean?

According to a 2009 study published the journal *Psychological Science,* this means that the SAT and many other standardized tests underpredict the performance of non-Asian minority students, and the performance of women in quantitative fields. In fact, the researchers posit that female students are, in fact, twenty points more competent in math than their SAT scores show. And non-Asian minority students are forty points more competent on the math and reading sections of the SAT than shown by their scores.

The brain is a wonderful organ. It starts working the moment you get up and does not stop until you get into the office.

—Robert Frost

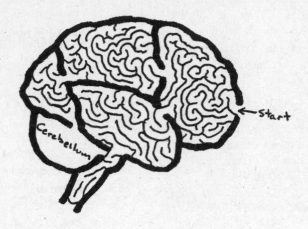

PIECE OF MIND: CEREBELLUM

The cerebellum is where we make sense of our senses—the independent observer that allows us to visualize our body in space and thus walk and hit fastballs.

Recent research also shows that the cerebellum helps us make sense of music. Drummers, especially, depend on it. Researchers asked subjects to reproduce rhythms of increasing complexity (given both audibly and visually) and watched with PET scans as the cerebellum sparkled. Just like timing a swing at an incoming fastball, the cerebellum extracts the timing from sound that we call rhythm. It's also used in pitch memory: Researchers played subjects a sequence of notes and asked whether the last note was the same as the first. Subjects whose MRI scans showed bright cerebellums more frequently responded correctly.

And so it's no surprise that musicians tend to have larger cerebellums than the population at large. This poses a chicken and the egg question: Are people with naturally larger cerebellums better at music and thus more likely to become musicians, or does musical training promote growth in the cerebellum?

ACTION AND FREE WILL

Despite the allegations of embarrassed sports stars and politicians, you and only you control your actions, right? In other words, it's your free will that allows you to grab that cup of coffee and every time you take a sip, you recognize you've done so. Right?

Um, "yes" wouldn't make a very good punch line, would it?

In fact, you *can* act without knowing it, you can *think* you've acted without actually doing so, and—this is the cool part— you can intend to act and think you've acted, without having moved at all.

Here's how:

The parietal cortex bookends an action. It's the home of intention and also evaluates an action's effect ("Hand, pick up that coffee! Yes, the hand has complied with my order!"). But a premotor circuit is what actually makes our muscles twitch ("Duh, OK boss"). Researchers zapped the parietal to create the phantom sensation of movement—subjects intended to move and thought they'd done so, but hadn't actually moved anything. Researchers then zapped premotor circuits— subjects moved without meaning to or knowing it.

Intention, Inaction, and Inebriation

In the coolest example of the placebo effect ever, researchers showed that intending to drink a beer and then believing you've done so can make you drunk, despite the sneaky substitution of a nonalcoholic beverage (in an experiment with obvious ethical and moral problems). On the other end of the health spectrum, it's unclear whether really, honestly intending to go for a run and then believing you've done so returns similar gains as actually going for a run (I plan extensive testing).

This might just seem like a freaky little factoid, but if your intention is split from your actions, then who is driving the bus? Contemplate the death of free will. Ohmmmmm.

DEBUNKED: MISDIAGNOSIS IMMUNITY

When a hospital he punked complained about his claims of misdiagnosis, Rosenhan engineered a further test of the hospital's powers of psychiatric diagnosis: He promised to send a number of fake patients to the hospital over the course of three months. During this time, the hospital evaluated 193 total patients. They labeled 41 of these patients as imposters and considered another 42 patients suspect.

In fact, Rosenhan hadn't sent any fake patients at all.

Critics of Rosenhan's experiments point out that psychiatric diagnosis depends on self-reporting. Perhaps a person who misreports hearing voices is as delusional and in need of treatment as the person who does, in fact, hear voices.

DEBUNKED: DIAGNOSIS BATSHIT

Clinically speaking, how do we know when a person's gone batshit? Hearing voices is a pretty good measure. And so in 1972, psychologist David Rosenhan wondered if patients would be admitted to psychiatric hospitals on the basis of voices alone. He recruited eight psychologically healthy confederates to find out. All eight tricked their way into mental hospitals based solely on their claims that indistinct voices were pronouncing the words *hollow, empty,* and *thud* in their heads.

Once inside, they acted perfectly normal, claiming the voices had left them. They took notes. One staff member considered this note taking pathological "writing behavior." The study's "patients" were released only after agreeing with staff psychiatrists that they were insane and starting antipsychotic medications. Their stays ranged from seven to fifty-two days.

Genius Tester #7: Missing Box

The four shapes that make up the upper image are repositioned to make the lower image. Both completed triangle puzzles are thirteen squares along the bottom and five along the right side. Only, the bottom shape has one blank square. How is this possible?

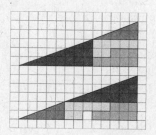

COFFEE AND CIGARETTES MAKE YOU SMARTER

You already know that your morning cup(s) of coffee make(s) you a better person: more alert, more outgoing, increasingly op-timistic, better looking, better smelling, nicer, etc. But did you know that coffee actually makes you smarter?

It does, really. But only for a short period of time, and when you come down, you're dumber than you were before taking that first sip (unless you drink more coffee!).

Studies show that caffeine increases the speed at which we process sensory information. And with luscious caffeine jouncing happily through our system, we make faster decisions based on these stimuli. In other words, we see faster and we act faster.

Cigarettes make us smarter too. Or at least their nicotine component does: It's been shown to boost short-term working memory and executive function. Nicotine patches have also been shown to combat some of the effects of Alzheimer's disease.

In other words, coffee makes us faster and nicotine makes us sharper. The crux is living long enough to enjoy these benefits.

You start chasing a ball and your brain immediately commands your body to "Run forward, bend, scoop up the ball, peg it to the infield," then your body says, "Who me?"

—Joe DiMaggio

Moderately drunk, coffee removes vapours from the brain,
occasioned by fumes of wine, or other strong liquors;
eases pains in the head, prevents sour belchings,
and provokes appetite.

—*England's Happiness Improved* (1699)

HOT OR NOT

Have you heard about HOTorNOT.com? It's a dating site that allows members to vote on other members' attractiveness. You carry your own attractiveness score with you and how hot you are becomes part of your profile. Researchers in the science of beauty and human attraction call this a data paradise. Here are some of the things researchers have been able to discover using HOTorNOT.com's magical numbers:

- Men are 240 percent more likely to accept a date offer than women.

- With each one-point gain in hotness (on a scale of 1 to 10), a person's chances of being accepted for a date increase by 130 percent.

- People who are themselves less attractive tend to under-value attractiveness in others, preferring to instead prioritize personality traits like kindness and sense of humor.

- As you'd expect, people are more likely to accept date offers from people with hotness scores greater than their own. But when the person requesting a date is more than four points hotter than the person being propositioned, the likelihood of acceptance tapers. Is this due to intimidation?

- Members' own attractiveness had no influence on how hot they perceived other members. In other words, less attractive members didn't delude themselves about their dates' attractiveness.

iDread

Alektorophobia: fear of chickens.

Wild Kingdom:
Chickens Like Models

If humans of all attractiveness levels recognize the same standards of beauty, the obvious question is *what about chickens*? To answer this important question, researchers in Stockholm taught male chickens to peck images of average human female faces. They then presented chickens with faces of varying beauties. Which faces did the chickens notice and thus peck more often? The same symmetrical, beautiful faces that male undergrads noticed.

Similar studies with similar results imply that animals across the evolutionary spectrum recognize and appreciate the same standards of beauty: Apparently symmetry implies genetic fitness.

GAME THEORY MAKE BRAIN BIG: THE SHORT-EST FUSE WINS THE BATTLE OF THE SEXES

Imagine a couple deciding if they'll go to the opera or to a football game (if needed, replace these bland stereotypes with specifics from your own relationship). Now imagine the possible outcomes: football together, football alone, opera together, and opera alone.

We can show this with the following grid (imagine the guy choosing a column and the lady choosing a row—they accept the outcome that gets two marks):

Now imagine each person has five "preference points" they can distribute among the four outcomes (again: football together, football alone, opera together, opera alone). And imagine, if you

will, that they prefer to go somewhere together. Imagine she *really* wants to go to the opera (four to one) while he's only somewhat more attached to football (three versus two). The grid 'would look like this:

The decision is obvious: If

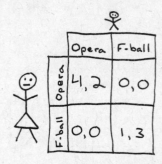

they both vote opera, they earn six total preference points (as opposed to four for 'football, and none if they split). But what if the guy feels as strongly about football as she does about opera:

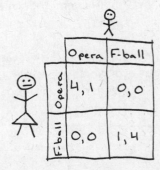

Now they're up the creek. Even with the opportunity to

collude (argue) they can't reach consensus and they don't want to risk choosing opposites, which would result in no preference points for anyone.

Mathematically, the cleanest solution is for them to use a commonly observed randomizing device: They flip a coin. Heads it's football and tails it's opera.

Actually, there's another option. One person can get mad. Imagine that through her anger, she's able to remove two of her total preference points—she threatens that if they fight over the decision, she won't have as much fun no matter what they end up doing. Now the grid looks like this, with the original preference points on top and the points if she gets mad below them:

	Opera	F-ball
Opera	4, 1	0, 0
	2, 1	-2, 0
F-ball	0, 0	1, 4
	-2, 0	-1, 4

The outcome: It's best for both if the guy gives in and goes to the opera before she gets mad. Thus they are guaranteed five preference points (but the poor dude never gets to the football game).

And the decision comes down to this: The person who is understood to be naturally capable of burning the most preference points and is most likely to burn them (i.e., can and will get the maddest) will earn their top-choice activity, every time.

ALGEBRAIC EIGHT-BALL: THE CHANCES THAT HE/SHE IS *"THE ONE"*

$$50\left[\left(\frac{2X + H + 25}{I_F + F + B_G + 25}\right)^{\left(\frac{A + \sqrt{T} + 25}{50}\right)}\right] = G_{ODDESS\%}$$

• X = How many of the following have you done: posted couples picture(s) to social networking website, chosen night with him/her over night with friends, sent him/her more than two updates during workday, skipped work to be with him/her, asked him/her for help, defended him/her from disparaging comments, deleted ex's contact information, wondered if he/she's the one on average of more than once per week.

• F = When you're awakened by the sound of his/her cacophonous snoring, catch him/her farting, or otherwise encounter stark evidence of basic humanity, you think: Enter from 1 to 10 with 1 being "aw, how terribly cute!" and 10 being "dear god, I'm dating/snogging/married to a diplodocus."

• B_G = Sum all the differences between the following numbers:

  • Your and their years of schooling.

  • A point for each ten points of difference in your and their estimated IQs.

  • On a scale from 1 to 10, your and their beauty.

  • On a scale from 1 to 10, your and their religious fervor.

  • On a scale from 1 to 10 (left to right), your and their politics.

• H = In hours, the estimated time before homicide of any form would occur in a trapped elevator containing you, him/her, and all your combined parents. Be realistic. Cap this at eight.

• I_F = When he/she asks an inconvenient favor, you: obey happily (1), obey with silent reservations (2), obey and gripe (3), disobey benignly (4), gripe and disobey (5).

• A = How old are you?

• T = Months you've known each other.

GODDESS% is the percentage chance that he or she's the one.

IF YOU SAY SO: MEMORABLE LIES, FORGETTABLE TRUTHS

If a friend tells you that a fuzzy picture of a mango is actually a banana (and you switch your opinion to believe him/her), the next day you will be more entrenched in your belief in the picture's banana-ness than you would be in its mango-ness had your friend simply confirmed the truth. It's as if −1 + 1 is greater than 1 + 1.

Cool, eh?

This is true to the point that even when the picture is made less fuzzy, gaining obvious mango-ness, you'll continue to see and believe banana if you've had time to solidify your trusted friend's belief—your entrenched wrong opinion resists the truth much more than a confirmed correct opinion.

It's as if believing a lie requires more dogmatic determination and thus holds tighter than the easy belief in the truth.

There are parallels to be made in human society.

THE EIGHT MENTAL DISORDERS OF 1857

This lithograph by Armand Gautier shows the eight mental disorders recognized (coincidentally) in the year that Hollywood was founded, including dementia, megalomania, acute mania, melancholia, idiocy, hallucination, erotic mania, and paralysis.

Wild Kingdom: Honor Among Thieves

Vampire bats may be bloodsuckers, but at least they play fair. These bats need to drink blood every night, but not every bat's lucky enough to sup a mammal's warm life force every night. These unsuccessful bats beg for blood barf. And bats to whom they've previously given are more likely to give in return.

Imagine your memory wiped clean every couple seconds. This is the case with Clive Wearing.

In 1985, Wearing, an accomplished musician, was the happily married director of the choir at Covent Garden. Then he contracted a virus that ate the portion of his brain responsible for coding new memories (losing much of his long-term memory, as well). Quoted in the *New Yorker,* his wife, Deborah, writes in her memoir *Forever Today,* "His ability to perceive what he saw and heard was unimpaired. But he did not seem to be able to retain any impression of anything for more than a blink. Indeed, if he did blink, his eyelids parted to reveal a new scene. The view before the blink was utterly forgotten."

Wearing stayed trapped in 1985, only things inexplicably changed in his world—a door was open instead of closed; Deborah was there, and then gone; things popped into and out of existence. But, almost cruelly, Wearing retained bits of *implicit* memory—somewhere in his unconscious he was able to grow and retain the impression that something was very wrong with him. And while he couldn't remember the names of prime ministers, he might blurt out "John Major Vehicle" when looking at a car with license plate JMV.

Also, somewhere in his less-than-conscious memory, Wearing held on to his ability to play music. Deborah writes, "Clive could sit down at the organ and play with both hands on the keyboard, changing stops, and with his feet on the pedals, as if this were easier than riding a bicycle."

And Wearing was not simply living in the moment of one bar of music, followed by the next bar, repeating the process until the bars ran out—he demonstrated phrasing that depended on knowledge of what had come before, where he was in the moment, and what would come after. In fact, Oliver Sacks writes in the *New Yorker* that while playing a piece of music, Wearing's memory would completely refrain from hitting the reset but, "without performance, the thread is broken, and he is thrown back once again into the abyss."

Self-Test: A Simple Memory Test

Look at this shape for ten seconds. Then try to draw it from memory.

GAME THEORY MAKE BRAIN BIG: EL FAROL BAR

Everyone loves the El Farol Bar in Santa Fe, New Mexico (especially W. Brian Arthur, who wrote this puzzle in 1994). That is, everyone loves the El Farol as long as it's not too crowded. If it's less than 60 percent full, it's more fun to be at the bar; if it's more than 60 percent full, it's more fun to stay home.

This puzzle has one more catch: Everyone has to decide whether to go or not go at exactly the same time, without communication.

You can probably see the catch-22 here.

So what's your best strategy? If you *were* allowed to communicate, what should you tell people about your choice?

Goldfish: "Just because I have a three-second memory, they think I'll stay content eating the same old fish flakes . . . Oh boy! Fish flakes!"

NANOTECHNOLOGY AND THE BLOOD-BRAIN BARRIER

Your body's a party and everybody's invited. Sure, your skin's a semicompetent bouncer, but once riffraff reaches the dance floor, they have the run of the place, diffusing across the porous walls of the vascular system and through the gaps between your body's relatively loose matrix of cells. So your body's evolved ways to deal with riffraff run amok, including straining them through the kidneys or liver, eliminating them via white-blood-cell hit men, and employing a continuous crew of contractors to repair any damage. If the riffraff overwhelm these safeguards, it's fairly easy for doctors to call in a cavalry of antibiotics or a good dose of activated charcoal.

Your brain, however, is a much more exclusive party, with a much better bouncer. Actually, the blood-brain barrier is made up of many bouncers (fatty endothelial cells) standing shoulder to shoulder (tight junctions). These corpulent bouncers stand so tightly together that even VIPs like oxygen can't squeeze around them, and must enter the party by virtue of being fat-soluble—they dissolve through the bouncers' fat, entering one side and exiting the other. (Don't worry: alcohol is fat-soluble too—the party can go on.) Any needed water-soluble substances like glucose and amino acids have to enter through doors made especially for them and them alone—these molecules pass through specialized channels, which act as miniature portals in the barrier.

With the very serious system of the blood-brain barrier in place, nothing unwanted gets in. Ever. And so the brain forgoes many of the body's safeguards, namely white blood cells, filtering, and much of the subcontractors that repair damage.

Of course, "never" is an overstatement. And this lack of other safeguards means that if even a little bit of riffraff crosses the blood-brain barrier, it can be very, very bad. Not only does the brain itself have few safeguards against infection, but the antibiotic cavalry can't get in the door to save the day. Also excluded by the blood-brain barrier are cancer drugs and drugs that target the HIV virus, which has evolved (as it is wont to do at a frightening pace) to gather and hide in the brain like plotting desperados in a west Texas cave.

Doctors have pioneered a

The Blood-Brain Barrier

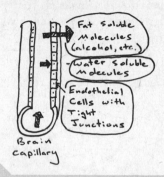

couple interventions to force drugs into the sack of the brain, including increasing osmotic pressure inside the skull, blasting the blood-brain barrier with ultrasound, and surgically implanting a time-release drug-delivery device inside the barrier. As you can imagine, none of these is much fun.

Enter nanotechnology.

In 2007, researchers at the University of Modena in Italy attached nanobubbles of biodegradable plastic to molecules that naturally pass through the blood-brain barrier and watched as the molecule/plastic pairs were recognized, vetted, and transported into the brain. Researchers hope this transport system will prove an effective method of smuggling drugs past the bouncers. Imagine many thousands of these molecule/plastic pairs and inside each biodegradable plastic bubble an antiretroviral molecule targeting HIV—no more hiding in the brain, pardners.

All the most acute, most powerful, and most deadly diseases, and those which are most difficult to be understood by the inexperienced, fall upon the brain.

—Hippocrates, circa 400 B.C.

THE DIET PARADOX: OFF-LIMITS IS OPEN SEASON

Imagine you're sitting in front of a pan of brownies. They're fresh. You're hungry. You're also on a diet, making these brownies strictly off-limits.

Do you eat the brownies?

It turns out that specifically because the brownies are off-limits, you're *more likely* to eat them. Researchers in Belgium demonstrated this by presenting subjects with an unhealthy snack and telling half the people not to eat it.

You can guess what happened.

Yep, those forbidden to eat the snack ate it more often. Researchers hypothesized that it's easier to break rules that seem artificially imposed than it is to break your own rules. (Perhaps if only the owner of a certain garden hadn't forbid a certain apple we'd all be sitting around naked sipping milk and honey.)

And so, paradoxically, being on a diet may make it more difficult to control your eating.

Nanotechnology and Brain-Computer Interface

Carbon nanotubes are like narrow noodles that happen to conduct electricity very well. As such, researchers hope they will lead to faster, smaller computers—and that they can be used to augment an existing operating system, namely the human brain. In 2007, researchers at the University of Trieste, Italy, grew neurons on single-wall carbon nanotubes and by stimulating the tubes caused the neurons to fire. The reverse seems promising: Electricity from firing neurons could be conducted through the tubes, and signals in these nanotubes could very plausibly be used to control a prosthetic limb (because the technology also has the potential to drive battlefield robots, funding is likely to continue).

ULTIMATE EVIL? NEUROIMAGING AS MARKET RESEARCH TOOL

You lie in an fMRI tunnel as a market researcher asks if you like his company's new product: a butt-kicking, gas-guzzling, V-12 SUV. You know you *shouldn't* like the earth-killing behemoth and so you respond *no*. But the researcher watches your amygdala and ventromedial prefrontal cortex light up—you may say no, but your pleasure centers are screaming *yeah, baby, yeah*. They want it and because humans are but weak pawns to our pleasure centers, you would buy it (if you could . . .). Your brain has betrayed you and the planet is doomed.

This is an example of the very scary field of neuromarketing—

looking inside the human brain to see which products light our lamps. The classic example of neuromarketing is a 2004 study of Coke versus Pepsi published in the journal *Neuron*. In this Pepsi Challenge, researchers fMRI-scanned the brains of sixty-seven participants as they blindly tasted the two soft drinks. Almost exactly half the brains lit up more for Coke and half lit up more for Pepsi.

But why then does Coke have a disproportionately large market share?

Wild Kingdom: Pufferfish

Beware the deadly pufferfish. Eating even a bite of the wrong part is 60 percent lethal. That's because the pufferfish is packed with tetrodotoxin, a powerful neurotoxin that elbows out sodium as the gatekeeper of the brain's ion channels. If sodium can't tell these ion channels to open and close, neurons can't fire and brain activity stops. This, as you might guess, is bad. There is no known antidote.

But administered very carefully, tetrodotoxin can cause muscle paralysis without affecting the brain—it can make your body seem dead while your mind's still alive. And as such, many hypothesize the chemical as the agent of Haitian voodoo zombiism.

The researchers tried the experiment again, this time telling participants beforehand which beverage they were drinking. Instead of simply lighting up pleasure centers, this time the brains showed activity in the lateral prefrontal cortex and hippocampus, areas of thought and memory. And three-quarters of the participants chose Coke (similar to Coke's market share). Basically, Coke's connection to our memories and expectations give it the edge, *even on a neural level.* Thus neuromarketers determined that Pepsi's recipe is fine, it's the branding that needs help.

If you think neuromarketing is unlikely to change the world, think again. Take, for example, the 2008 presidential election, in which John McCain failed to light the amygdalas of enough registered voters. What could he have said to create more positive brain vibes? Did he need to hold tight to the image of happy warrior or was he right to go negative? To what issues did voters most viscerally respond and which positions were the most popular? You can be sure that future candidates will know, having tested their platforms and personalities directly on the brains of voters.

The French Diet

Most people rate the food in Paris higher than the food in Chicago. But Parisians eat less than Chicagoans. Why?

In fact, the French eat less than Americans because they listen to their bodies' consumption cues: When they're full, they stop. Americans are more likely to rely on external cues: When our TV show's over, we stop. Or when the plate's empty, we stop.

PIECE OF MIND: AMYGDALA

The two almond-sized lobes of the amygdala attach fearful emotions to memories on their way into storage.

Because the amygdala recognizes negative emotion, people with damaged amygdalae can be especially docile. For example, researchers showed subjects images of aggressive and/or frightening faces and found that subjects with damaged amygdalae sat passively, while control subjects recoiled. And without its connection to the hypothalamus, people with damaged amygdalae are unable to learn from their emotions: What is safe and what is dangerous remains a mystery.

Interestingly, young people have more volatile amygdalae than adults, while adults have a stronger connection between the amygdala and the hippocampus. This means that when a high chair tips backward, a child may experience more fear than its parents, but parents and not children learn more from the experience.

Eye Hack: Satire on False Perspectives

How many errors in perspective can you find in this 1754 engraving by William Hogarth? Five of the many errors are listed at the back of this book.*

Whoever makes a DESIGN, without the Knowledge of PERSPECTIVE will be liable to such Absurdities as are shewn in this Frontispiece.

* Note: If you're having trouble seeing this image clearly, just hop on Google Images and search "Hogarth Satire on Perspective" for a bigger version.

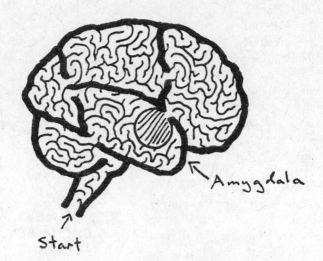

Amygdala

Start

FUGGEDABOUTIT

If only you could ditch that traumatic memory, that craving, that debilitating fear of ventriloquist dummies (automatonophobia)! But these tendencies are so deeply ingrained that try as you might, you can't dig them out.

Maybe you can drug them out.

The process of recalling a memory is like a rolling snowball—a trigger provides the first ball, which then rolls through various parts of your brain picking up the additional elements it needs to become a full memory.

The molecule PKMzeta rolls the ball. Actually, when a trigger hits your brain, PKMzeta chooses the paths it takes, allowing it to gather relevant info. And the more frequently you remember something, the more you reinforce these PKMzeta pathways, making the memory easier to access next time. Without PKMzeta, you can roll a snowball and it won't pick up anything.

Now imagine being able to block this PKMzeta exactly when you want. This is what the chemical ZIP does. When researchers injected ZIP into rats, the rats forgot what they'd learned about electrical shocks in the floors of their cages; another injection of ZIP made rats forget a sour taste (perhaps another injection would help the rats forget why they're pissed off at the researchers).

With more work, ZIP could make you forget to smoke when you sit at a bar, forget the traumatic memory of seeing the movie *Spice World,* or forget the time many years ago that you were savaged by that evil ventriloquist dummy.

But given the opportunity, which memories should we block? Traumatic as it was, aren't we better off remembering our dread of *Spice World* so that we can adjust our future behavior? And couldn't removing memories also wipe out our morality and conscience, developed over years of remembering the consequences of our actions?

BAD MONKEY. NO CUCUMBER.

A study at the Yerkes National Primate Research Center in Atlanta found that monkeys were perfectly happy to work for cucumber slices. That is, until one monkey was given grapes. Then the other monkeys stopped working for cucumbers and started nursing a grudge.

Dogs do the same, only their taste isn't quite as discriminating: A dog will "shake hands" for a compliment until it sees another dog getting a food reward for the same task. Then the first dog holds out for food. But the reward can be kibble or filet mignon.

Similar experiments have yet to be performed with professional athletes in their years of free agency.

Canst thou not minister to a mind diseased,
Pluck from the memory a rooted sorrow,
Raze out the written troubles of the brain?

—Shakespeare, *Macbeth,* act 5, scene 3

WILD KINGDOM: HOOKNOSE JACK

A pirate? No: a coho salmon breeding strategy. In coho society, the hooknoses are large, fierce salmon that fight each other for access to females, while jacks are small, fast salmon that snog the females while the hooknoses are accomplishing said fighting.

Interestingly, female salmon prefer the jacks, spending more time preparing their nests and ovipositing (dropping eggs) when in jacks' presence. But in order to avoid mating with winning hooknoses, they have to spend energy escaping. And so both coercion (hooknose) and cooperation (jack) work for male salmon.

GAME THEORY MAKE BRAIN BIG: PIRATE PUZZLE

Argh, matey! 'Tis a treasure chest fulla 100 gold pieces, and five pirates for to split it! For truth, the pirates each be fiercer than the next. And so the fiercest

be telling the rest how the gold be split. If the vote's a tie or better, the gold be split so. But if the vote be nay, the fiercest pirate be thrown o'erboard and the next fiercest pirate be proposing how the gold be split. (And all else equal, a pirate be liking to throw another o'erboard.)

How should the fiercest pirate be proposin' to split the 100 gold pieces?

BLINDSIGHT

TN walked down the cluttered hallway, sidestepping a garbage can, a tripod, a stack of paper, and several boxes. It required tricky footwork.

Oh, and TN was blind.

A pair of strokes had completely destroyed his visual lobes, leaving his sight not "very blurry" or "black with flashes" but completely and profoundly absent. But his eyes continued to gather and transmit input, and researchers believe this input filtered into alternate brain channels for interpretation.

For example, when researchers showed TN images of fearful faces, TN cringed as a sighted subject would . . . without consciously registering that he'd seen anything at all. Sure enough, cells in the retina connect with circuits that run directly through the amygdala—TN, and perhaps everyone, interprets the emo-tional content of a visual stimulus without the intermediate step of actually "seeing" it. Perhaps TN's amygdala also felt the emotional presence of trash cans cluttering the hallway?

Or maybe rats hold the answer.

Deep within the rat midbrain are neurons that accept input from the eyes, and fire when special conditions exist. In rats, these triggers include passing a landmark, head orientation,

Wild Kingdom:
Eight Arms, Zero Blind Spot

Because the octopus's optic nerve attaches to the back of its eyes' receptor cells instead of passing through them, the octopus has no blind spot.

and—most interestingly for TN—being close to a border. Norwegian researchers (presumably taking advantage of the abundant supply of eponymous brown rats) watched midbrain rat neurons fire when the rodents scurried close to walls. Perhaps similar cells helped TN recognize when he was close to obstacles.

Blindsight Video

Search "blindsight" online to find video of TN navigating the hallway, or visit the lead researcher's website at www .beatricedegelder.com.

Eye Hack: Blind Spot

Close your right eye and look at the L. Slowly move the page closer until the R disappears. Repeat, closing your left eye and looking at the R. Because there are no receptors where the optical nerve connects to the retina, you have this small blind spot, which is normally filled by information from your other eye.

R   L

PIECE OF MIND: OCCIPITAL LOBE

Directly opposite our eyes at the very back of the brain is the occipital lobe, where we process sight information. (Were we meant to have eyes in the back of our head?) Other than its obvious role in transforming the pops and clicks of electrical stimulus from our eyes into goodies recognizable by our consciousness, the occipital lobe stores the color tags associated with memories. Researchers showed this by presenting subjects with shapes—some colored and some not—and then asking subjects to remember the colors of the various shapes. PET scans showed their occipital lobes crackling when they remembered colored shapes; not so when they remembered the uncolored shapes.

Damage to the occipital lobe can result in its including bits of misinformation with the material it sends to our consciousness. We call these hallucinations.

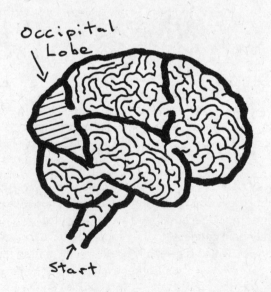

Occipital Lobe

Start

INTUITION TRUMPS REASON: THE IOWA GAMBLING TASK

In the Iowa Gambling Task, a participant is presented with four facedown decks of cards. He or she can flip over cards from any deck. Most cards earn a reward and some cards incur a penalty. Of the four decks, some are better (contain more reward-earning cards) than others. Over time, participants should learn which decks are best and start flipping cards from only the highest-paying decks. The test is thought to measure the emotional component of learning, or intuition—based on reward and punishment, participants begin to "feel" which decks are best and worst.

There are many, many cool things that have been done with the Iowa Gambling Task. Here are a few:

• Most healthy participants take between forty and fifty flips to recognize good and bad decks and then stick to the good ones. But galvanic skin tests, like those of a lie detector, show that after only about ten flips, participants start to show stress responses

Iowa Gambling at Home

A quick online search turns up a couple places where you can test your own prowess at the Iowa Gambling Task.

as their hands hover above bad decks. We know a bad deck before we're aware of it.

• The orbitofrontal cortex processes the emotion of reward and punishment as it relates to decision-making. When you wince after a bad choice, that's the orbitofrontal cortex at work. People with brain damage in this region, while cognitively unimpaired, are devoid of the emotions of good and bad choices. And they show no galvanic skin response to impending bad choices on the Iowa Gambling Task. In fact, these people will sometimes continue to choose cards from bad decks long after they're aware that they're losing money.

- Dumber is better. It turns out that a college education is a predictor of *poorer* performance on the Iowa Gambling Task. Though unproven, most people think this effect is due to higher education's emphasis on rational decision-making at the expense of emotion-based decisions. In other words, college squashes our intuition. Education can also increase our confidence in false beliefs—when an educated person thinks he or she has found a pattern, or has made a good-deck/bad-deck judgment, he or she is likely to have confidence in this evaluation . . . even if it's wrong.

Eye Hack: Faubert-Herbert Illusion

A very slick packaging trick has allowed this book to include an animated spinning wheel. Look just below the wheel and blink rapidly.

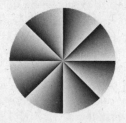

- Is the Iowa Gambling Task really a test of intuition? Researchers made participants take the test while performing another cognitively challenging task. If the Gambling Task required thought (as opposed to intuition) this mentally overtaxed group should've taken longer to catch on. They didn't, implying that cognitive learning and emotion-based learning don't compete for brain space, and that the Iowa Gambling Task requires something other than the traditional idea of conscious thought.

- When gambling for play money, cocaine users significantly underperformed nonusers. But when the money got real, cocaine users took more time than nonusers, but eventually scored the same.

• Participants with amnesia failed to develop a preference for good decks. This implies that intuition, while somewhat independent of cognition, continues to depend on memory. Our intuition remains built on experience.

• A kid's version of the test, called the Hungry Donkey Test, challenges kids to pick the door that consistently gives the donkey the most apples.

OTHER COOL NEUROPSYCH TESTS

There are literally thousands of neuropsychological tests competing with one another for adoption, like Darwin's finches for seeds (and with equal levels of specialization). Here are but a few of the heavy hitters:

WISCONSIN CARD-SORTING TASK: If the Iowa Gambling Task measures intuition, then the test developed in its beer- and cheese-loving northeastern neighbor is its opposite, measuring cognition (specifically attention, working memory, and visual processing). In it, par-

ticipants learn through trial and error the rules of how to match symbol cards.

TOVA: The Test of Variables of Attention measures the ability to sustain attention and is used most often in diagnosing ADHD. Basically, it's a god-awfully boring test that requires constant vigilance for 22.6 minutes. In it, a participant watches a screen and clicks a button when a tiny square shows up (infrequently). An auditory version does the same with a tone. It's boring to even think about.

FOUR CHOICE RESPONSE TIME: Would you have survived a high-noon shoot-out on the dusty streets of Tombstone? The Four Choice Response Time test is a good predictor. Quick! In which quadrant did the plus sign appear? Hit the button! Draw! And do you want to know why there are old gunslingers and bold gunslingers but no old, bold gunslingers? It's because reaction time peaks in young adulthood and slows down as you age.

LEXICAL DECISION TASK: Word or pseudoword? Ready, set, go: Trud! Barn! Dragmar! Nurse! Doctor! Flimp! Change! Your reaction times in hitting a word/

nonword buzzer determine your *semantic memory,* or how quickly you recall things from your language quiver. One cool piece of the Lexical Decision Task is the role of priming: You were quicker to recognize "Doctor" because it was preceded by "nurse" (had it been preceded by "horse" you would have been slower).

THE STROOP TASK: You will more quickly and accurately read a green-colored word "green" than you will read a red-colored word "green." The TV show *Nova* used the Stroop Task to show climbers getting loopier and loopier as they ascended Everest. That wacky hypoxia!

To try these tests and more, visit pebl.sourceforge.net.

THE TRANSFORMATIVE POWER OF THE UNEXPECTED

If you're going to open someone's head, you might as well make the most of it, right? This must be what surgeons at U Penn thought. To control the tremors and rigidity of Parkinson's, they commonly insert small, battery-powered devices called neuro-stimulators deep within patients' midbrains. Since patients have to be awake during the surgery, why not also use microelectrodes to measure the firing rates of dopamine-releasing neurons in patients' substantia nigra during a simulated gambling task?

Here's what they found:

Neurons turned on dopamine when subjects won simulated money. And the dopamine release was proportionate to the amount of money they won. No surprise. But when winning was unexpected—bang!—dopamine skyrocketed, with "winnings" in the brain disproportionate to the amount of winnings in the gambling task.

In other words, while meeting our expectations has a slightly reinforcing effect on our emotional memory, and thus future behavior, something unexpected makes us drastically adjust our worldview. In the mathematics of evolution, it's as if an expected result—no matter how large—is just another dot on an existing curve. But even a small, unexpected result forces us to redraw these curves entirely.

And in the substantia nigra of patients undergoing conscious neurosurgery, we can see how.

COOL NEUROSURGERY PAST AND PRESENT: CONSCIOUS NEUROSURGERY

A tumor can grow anywhere in the brain. And because each brain region has a specific function, where a tumor grows determines its symptoms: Do you lose sensation, speech, memory, movement?

And as you might imagine, removing a brain tumor is rather unpleasant. Tumors aren't simply hanging fruit that can be snipped at their stem and plucked out whole; they're intermingled with other tissue, with a gradient rather than a clear line between tumor edge and healthy tissue. So when neurosurgeons remove tumors, it's difficult to know exactly when to stop cutting. They'd like to remove as much as possible, but without cutting away useful bits of your brain. They decide when to stop by the simple method of poking and checking—as long as a conscious patient retains function, a surgeon can keep cutting.

Wünderdrug

What's this wünderdrug that masks the pain of invasive brain surgery while allowing a patient to stay conscious and coherent? Actually, the drug's been about 4.5 billion years in R&D and is called *nothing*. The human brain feels no pain.

EYE HACK: STEREOGRAM

Unfocus your eyes as you stare at the following image. Force the blurred white dots to overlap until they come back into focus, one atop the other. In the resulting 3-D image, which row is farthest back? Which jumps farthest off the page? Our brains usually meld the two, slightly different images that come from each eye to create the appearance of three dimensions. By "layering" one dot atop another, you provide the brain with two slightly different images, which combined look three-dimensional.

Crocodile Tears

The fifth cranial nerve controls the face's mucous membranes: snot, tears, saliva, etc. And when this cranial nerve is damaged, liquids can go awry. In the neurological disorder known as crocodile tears, patients cry when they eat—they produce tears instead of saliva.

HANDWRITING ANALYSIS

Why is doctors' handwriting illegible? In fact, it's not *all* doctors whose handwriting is scribblier than the norm—it's male specialists, and they share illegibility with male executives in other professions. Why? Is it because they see themselves as important to the point of dismissing the mundane task of written notes to the proletariat? Though there's significant debate as to whether our slants and curlicues correlate to our personalities, graphologists say they do. Here's a small sampling of graphology basics:

- Writing that slants to the right indicates an extravert, leaning forward into life. The opposite is true of a left slant, and dead vertical writing is a sign of practicality.

- The larger the letters, the larger the need for attention.

- The wider the space between words, the more ponderous the person.

- People who write legibly want to be understood, though hyperlegibility is the mark of someone beating you over the head with their message.

Now, can you use these clues to match the following people to their handwriting samples below? (No fair reading the content for clues!)

PEOPLE

Walt Whitman, Fidel Castro, Jack the Ripper, the Zodiac killer, Mahatma Gandhi, Charles Darwin, Jane Austen, Abraham Lincoln.

HANDWRITING

1

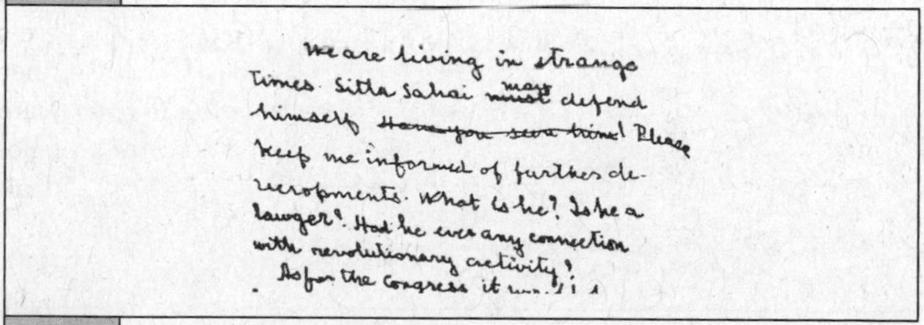

we are living in strange times. Sitta Sahai may defend himself. Have you seen him! Please keep me informed of further developments. What is he? Is he a lawyer? Had he ever any connection with revolutionary activity? . As for the Congress it ..... ! ! !

2

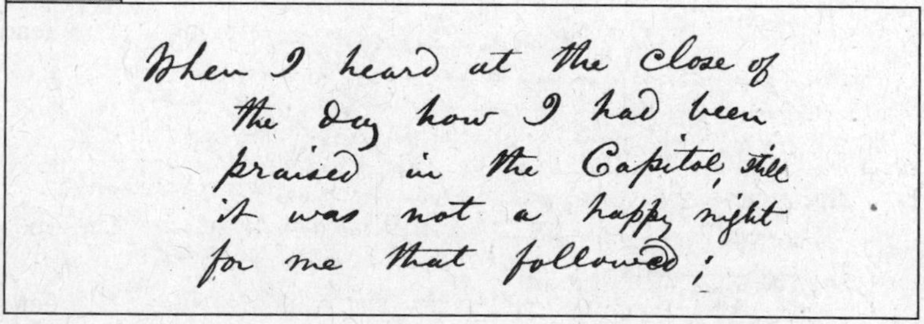

When I heard at the close of the Day how I had been praised in the Capitol, still it was not a happy night for me that followed;

3

If you like, give me a
ten dollars bill green american, in the letter, because
never, I have not seen a
ten dollars bill green american and I would like
to have one of them.

4

Four score and seven years ago our fathers
brought forth, upon this continent, a new nation, con-
ceived in Liberty, and dedicated to the proposition
that all men are created equal.

5

We told Mr. B. Lefroy that if the weather did
not prevent us, we should certainly come & see you tomorrow;
& bring Cassy, trusting to your being so good as to give her
a dinner about one o'clock, that we might be able to
be with you the earlier & stay the longer — but unless
Cassy has choice of the Fair or Wyards, it must be supposed
that she has preferred the former, which we trust will not
greatly affront you; — if it does, you may hope that some
little Anna hereafter may revenge the insult by a similar

6

This is the Zodiac speaking
I though you would need a
good laugh before you
hear the bad news
you wont get the *and i*
news for a while yet *cant*
PS could you print *do a*
this new cipher *thing*
in your frunt paper *with*
I get awfully lonely *it!*
when I am ignored,
So lonely I could
do my *Thing !!!!!!*

Des July Aug
Sept Oct = 7

7

Mr Such
Sor I send you half the
Kidne Stook from one woman
I have recovered it for you to ther piece
fried and ate it was very nise I
may send you the blady knay that
took it out if you only wate a whil
longer.

8

I am much obliged for the
gift of your beautifully got-up book
on the vicissitudes of S. Africa,
and for your other prezzs

Handwriting Forensics

While handwriting analysis can help construct psychological profiles, perhaps of more use is the more straightforward task of matching samples to suspects. Consider the case of one-month-old Peter Weinberger, who was kidnapped in 1956 from his home in Westbury, on Long Island. His kidnapper scrawled a ransom note in green ink. FBI handwriting experts noticed the kidnapper's lowercase "m" looked like a sideways "z" and searched more than two million public documents looking for a match. A probation officer in Brooklyn found it in a document written by thirty-one-year-old auto mechanic Angelo LaMarca: his m's looked like z's. After questioning, LaMarca confessed and was convicted.

CRANIAL NERVE MNEMONICS

Memorizing the paths of the twelve cranial nerves is a major reason more people don't become doctors. Calling these pathways "messy" is an understatement. It's as if a small house were built and wired in 1920 and then as new rooms were added, the electrician simply extended, branched, and rerouted the existing wiring—sometimes snaking circuitous and intensely illogical routes through the house, so that instead of a wire traveling from the circuit box to a bulb in the kitchen, the wire first travels through the attic. If you saw how the house was originally built and then extended, the paths of these wires might make sense, but looking at the modern house, the wiring simply looks like a mess. This is exactly what happened in the course of human evolution—our brain's wiring is one giant workaround (as Neil Shubin points out in his book *Your Inner Fish*).

The first step in learning the paths of these cranial nerves is learning their names, which med students commonly do with the use of mnemonics. In order, the nerves are the olfactory, optic, oculomotor, trochlear, trigeminal, abducens, facial, vestibulocochlear/auditory, glossopharyngeal, vagus, accessory (spinal accessory), and hypoglossal.

And here are common mnemonics used to remember these nerves:

- Ongoing ordeals of trampoline tragedies, America's Funniest Videos, go video! Saget hour!

- On old Olympus' towering tops a friendly Viking grew vines and hops

- Olympic opium occupies troubled triathletes after finishing Vegas gambling vacations still high

- Ooo truly there are five very gorgeous vixens awaiting him

- Oh once one takes the anatomy final very good vacations are heavenly

Genius Tester #8: Houses and Utilities

There are three houses and three utilities: electric, water, and gas. Each house is linked to all three utilities, but no lines cross, none is shared, and none passes through houses or utilities. Can you draw all nine lines? Hint: The world is not flat.

KNOX BOX

Immigrants passing through Ellis Island in the early 1900s

were given a series of tests to prove their fitness as citizens. Prospective immigrants were turned back for tuberculosis, cholera, nail fungus, and especially an eye infection known as trachoma. They were also turned back for mental deficiency.

But how were immigration officials to test mental acuity in a population that spoke little English?

Dr. Howard Knox solved this problem with five small black cubes.* He lined up four cubes on a table in front of the person being tested and then, like the game Simon Says, used the fifth cube to tap patterns on the four resting cubes. Using sign language, he asked prospective immigrants to reproduce the patterns by tapping the correct cubes. Here is the sequence he used:

a. 1,2,3,4

b. 1,2,3,4,3

c. 1,2,3,4,2

d. 1,3,2,4

e. 1,3,4,2,3,1

Respectively, Knox said these sequences should be able to be performed by a four, five, six, eight, and eleven year old. In a 1914 article charmingly titled "The Moron and the Study of

---

* Not to be confused with the Mr. Knox best known as the perpetually tongue-tied straight man to Theodor Geisel's famous fox.

Alien Defectives," Knox wrote, "I present this paper, based on tests which I have made on over 4,000 suspected defectives in the last eighteen months . . . all were considered sufficiently near the required standard to be allowed to pass, except 400 certified as feeble-minded and (in a few cases) as imbeciles."

Can you, your friends, and your loved ones all pass the 1,3,4,2,3,1 test required for admission to the United States?

COOL NEUROSURGERY PAST AND PRESENT: CORPUS CALLOSOTOMY

In some types of severe epileptic seizures, electrical activity bounces between the brain's hemispheres like a ricocheting bullet. Neurosurgeons know how to stop the bullet short: They snip the connection between the hemispheres. The procedure's known as a corpus callosotomy, and done right it actually has fewer side effects than you might imagine.

Interestingly, one side effect is that a patient may not be able

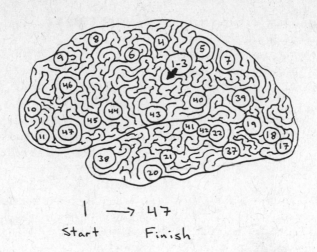

I → 47

Start Finish

to read words he sees on his far left side. Because this far left visual stimulus crosses and is recognized by the right visual cortex, it can't get to Broca's or Wernicke's area in the left side of the brain for processing into comprehensible form. (If a word's on the viewer's right, the *left* visual cortex sees it, and can send it within the same hemisphere to Broca and Wernicke.)

A related side effect is being unable to name an unseen object placed in the left hand. Again, the sensory information crosses and arrives in the right brain, but then the signal can't travel to Broca or Wernicke to pull up the corresponding vocabulary.

PIECE OF MIND: BRODMANN AREAS

In 1909, Korbinian Brodmann stained the brain.

Using a technique called the Nissl stain, Brodmann was able to see groupings of interconnected cells and cell types within the five lobes of the cerebral cortex. These clumped cells proved to be like the tools of a Swiss Army knife, each specialized for a different processing purpose. And by observing patients with brain damage in different locations, Brodmann was able to determine the functions of these areas. While they've been refined over the years, the essential designations of Brodmann's areas have changed little. Highlights include the primary motor cortex (4), primary visual cortex (17), and auditory cortex (41–42).

Psy-Op: Infarction

What does a spider use to weave its web? Spell this word out loud. Now say it three more times while picturing a web.

Wait. Wait. Wait.

Now, what do cows drink? Can you find the word? No?

BRAIN SWEAT

We know the mouth is a useful orifice for venting our feelings: If we're "hot," speaking our anger can help us "cool off." And so the bigger the mouth, the better the cooling, right?

Actually, yes.

When our brain gets hot, we cool it through the mouth, and the best way to cool through the mouth is by yawning.

Researchers showed this by cooking parakeets.

OK, they stopped short of actually cooking them, but they found that when temperature increased, the parakeet yawn rate doubled (there was no description of researchers' yawn rates).

This fits with our understanding of yawning as a symptom of thermoregulatory diseases. We yawn in the lead-up to epileptic seizure (hot electricity in the brain). Yawning can also presage migraines. In multiple sclerosis, the myelin surrounding nerve axons is damaged, and hot electricity leaks out—and many MS patients experience bouts of excessive yawning.

And it's no coincidence that we also yawn when we're tired: Exhaustion and sleep-deprivation increase deep brain temperature.

YOUR BRAIN ON SPACE

The body spends a good deal of energy forcing fluids to go up. Otherwise you'd have very big feet. But cerebrospinal fluid has no pump. Instead, after it's created in the brain, it sinks downward where eventually it's reabsorbed by your blood vessels (or, some posit, into the lymph system).

Thank you, gravity.

But what happens when there is no gravity? Wouldn't excess fluid just stay in the brain and create all kind of problems? Interestingly, it seems we're evolutionarily prepared for space travel (insert ancient astronaut theory here). In conditions of reduced gravity, our brain produces less fluid.

Additional effects of zero gravity include reports of space euphoria akin to Buddhist realization of the interconnectedness of the universe ("It comes through to you so powerfully that you're the sensing element for Man," said astronaut Rusty Schweikart).

AUTISM AND LEGOS

Is your father an engineer (think bridges and robots, not trains)? How about your grandfather? If so, you have an increased risk of autism. And here's an interesting fact: Both autistics and their engineer fathers/grandfathers are better than the average bear at the block design portion of the standard IQ test (block design measures spatial visualization). This means that kids who are especially adept at building with LEGOs whose fathers/grandfathers are engineers, are, statistically speaking, up the autism creek sans paddle. (Concerned parents may mail LEGO sets to this author via Three Rivers Press, especially TECHNIC sets from the late 1980s.)

MALES' RAT-BRAINED NAVIGATION

Imagine you're navigating a three-dimensional maze. Believe it or not, in this situation, both men and women think. However, women think with the distinctly

The Knowledge

Before a London cabbie is licensed to drive a black cab, he (or, very infrequently, she) must pass a test known as The Knowledge. The test requires knowing almost 25,000 streets as well as the points of interest along these streets including squares, clubs, hospitals, hotels, theaters, embassies, government and public buildings, railway stations, police stations, courts, important places of worship, cemeteries, crematoria, parks and open spaces, sports and leisure centers, places of learning, restaurants, and historic buildings. Average preparation for The Knowledge takes thirty-four months and passing the test itself usually requires upward of twelve attempts.

human right prefrontal cortex, while men use the rat-brain navigational instincts of their left hippocampus (according to fMRI studies). Basically, what this means is that while men efficiently snuffle around the corridors, rationally and analytically memorizing each branching path, women look at the map. And if the map is unclear, they ask directions (not to reinforce a pop stereotype or anything).

Interestingly, London's taxi drivers (who are expert at navigating a three-dimensional maze) have enlarged hippocampi compared with the general population. The longer the cabbie's been driving, the bigger the hippocampus.

PIECE OF MIND: PARIETAL LOBE

With the traditional thinking gesture, you scratch your parietal lobe. This lobe makes sense of space, both recognizing the dimensions and features of space around us and keeping track of how our body is positioned in this space. It also helps us slap coordinates on things we perceive. It's as if the parietal lobe holds a three-dimensional graph of our surroundings, dotted with points that represent all the things we're aware of (and many we're not).

In fact, it holds a couple of these graphs: certainly one based on visual input and another based on auditory input, and perhaps more graphs for more senses (does our parietal hold a map of smell positions?). And based on its confidence in these maps, it can switch from one to the other like Predator switching from thermal to ultraviolet vision. In most cases our visual input most accurately captures the dimensions of our surroundings, but if sound is up and sight is down, our parietal switches to its auditory map.

MRI studies show that women tend to have proportionally greater parietal lobe gray matter than do men, while men have increased parietal surface area. This may explain males' relative aptitude (and females' relative ineptness) on mental rotation tasks.

GAME THEORY MAKE BRAIN BIG: NASH BARGAINING GAME

You and I are going to split $100. We each write the amount we demand on a slip of paper and

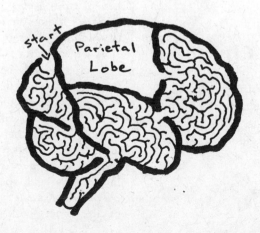

then we show each other the demands. If our demands, added together, are less than or equal to $100, we split it as proposed and we both get paid. If the sum of our demands is greater than $100, neither of us gets jack.

What's the solution?

Melencolia I

This famous 1514 engraving by the old master Albrecht Dürer shows a depressive genius.

THE BRAIN-WORKS OF RELIGIOUS CONVICTION AND ECSTASY

What happens when you die? What's right and wrong? What's the purpose of life? Aaaaarrghhh!

Chill out, God has the answers. And the religious part of your brain knows it.

The anterior cingulated cortex is the human home of anxiety. And it's increasingly chill in people with religious conviction. In fact, this anxiety center is quieter in people with *any* strong convictions that answer big questions, including conservative political ideologies. (This isn't necessarily a bad thing: It seems that many people could benefit from a chill pill shoved into their brain's anxiety center.)

And do you remember the story of Siddhārta Gautama sitting cross-legged beneath the bodhi tree, when his self suddenly merged with the universe? Researchers at the University of Missouri found that this "selfless" religious ecstasy is seen in the brain as reduced activity in the right parietal lobe. Likewise, people with damage to this area of the brain—perhaps due to motorcycle accidents or sacred fig whackage—are more likely to experience selfless religious experience.

Because it's impossible to gather a group of subjects and then prescribe half of them a steady diet of religious conviction, it's very difficult to separate which is cause and which is effect in these cases: Does religion quiet anxiety centers, or are people with quiet anxiety centers drawn to religion? The same is the case with parietal lobe damage and selfless religious ecstasy: Are people with quiet parietals likely to experience selfless ecstasy, or does this ecstasy quiet the parietal?

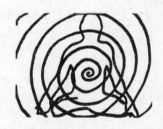

The Meditative Mind

fMRI studies show that brain regions responsible for regulating emotion are larger in long-term meditators. Again, does meditation grow your gray matter or are people with overdeveloped emotion regulation centers drawn to meditation?

iDread

Papaphobia:
fear of the pope.

SELF-TEST

Read the statements below and use a pencil to score each question's accuracy in describing your thoughts or behaviors, with one being "very inaccurate" and five being "very accurate." Flip to the back of the book for interpretation.

1. I like to follow a regular schedule.

2. I dislike loud music.

3. I oppose authority.

4. I want things to proceed according to plan.

5. I let others down.

6. I have no sympathy for criminals.

7. I respect authority.

8. I don't care about rules.

I CHOOSE MY CHOICE

In 1956, psychologist Jack Brehm asked housewives to rank how much they wanted certain household items. Then Brehm asked them to choose between items they'd rated equally desirable, perhaps a vacuum cleaner and a dishwasher. Then Brehm asked the housewives to rank all the items again. In this second pass, housewives who'd chosen dishwashers found them even more desirable than they had in the first round. And they found the item they decided against—perhaps the vacuum cleaner—less desirable than before.

This is a classic example of post-rationalization: Of course you made the correct choice between the dishwasher and the vacuum cleaner, because look at their (new) difference in desirability! But does forcing a person to make a tough choice between two objects clarify a preference that already exists, or does this choosing *create* the preference, itself?

Both, it seems.

Researchers in London watched participants' brains as they pondered and then rated the desirability of various vacation destinations. Then researchers forced them to choose between vacations they'd rated equally desirable.

But researchers could've predicted which vacations the participants would choose—they'd charted how brightly each destination lit each participant's caudate nucleus, a region of the brain linked to anticipating rewards—and more often than not, a participant's choice reflected what their caudate nucleus already knew. So, forcing a choice between similar vacations brought existing preferences to light.

Then participants got back in the scanner and rated the destinations again. Like the housewives, participants' caudate nuclei lit *brighter than the first time* for the vacations they picked, and were dimmer than the first time when imagining the desirability of the vacations they decided against. And so, a person's choice also creates—or at least solidifies—a preference.

Eye Hack: Café Wall Illusion

Look at this jumble! Now look again. The horizontal lines are all parallel.

FEAR-THEN-RELIEF PRISONER COMPLIANCE

Mountain climbers know the most dangerous part of the climb is the descent. Once you've tagged the summit, not only are you tired, but you're relieved, too. The scary part of the climb is over and you can relax. Then your heel skids and you tumble.

The same is true of stubborn prisoners. Despite the logic that fear should create compliance, a Polish summary of five studies found it was when fear *ceased* that prisoners started following orders. The researchers explained their findings in part by noting that fear claims enough cognitive energy that scared prisoners are unable to rationally process requests. When scared, the prisoners simply said no and stuck to it, but when experiencing relief, they both evaluated requests rationally and did so through rose-colored glasses. (Notice the model requires that fear be present at a certain point—take *that* Geneva Conventions!)

GAME THEORY MAKE BRAIN BIG: SIGNALING STRATEGIES IN BRIDGE AND IN JOB INTERVIEWS

My grandmother was a wonderful Scandinavian Lutheran woman who just happened to experience a certain bloodlust when playing bridge. To her, what happened in the game certainly did not stay in the game. The same is true of game theorists. To them, bridge is a clean-ish microcosm in which to study "Bayesian signaling games," in which partners attempt to communicate through the veil of incomplete information—you know what cards you have, and through your bidding and actions, I attempt to infer what you have.

This game becomes life when you consider a job interview. In it, there are two players: The employer and the applicant. During the interview, the applicant holds the information and tries to signal competence and motivation, while the employer tries to infer the cards the applicant holds: What's the applicant's true skill level? There are ways the applicant signals his or her true skill: a university degree, articulate and intelligent conversation, lack of Cheez Whiz on the interview tie, etc.

The first—a university degree —is an interesting signal, and one that implies more than a certain level and type of training. Economically, the primary reasons to earn a degree are expected salary and personal bet-

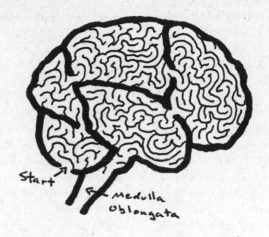

Start

Medulla
Oblongata

terment, and the factors standing in the way of the degree are tuition and effort. If required effort is extremely high (i.e., if your mental capacity doesn't naturally stretch to the course requirements), it may not make economic sense to complete the degree. So in a job interview, having a degree implies that you're skilled enough to have made the economic choice to earn the degree in the first place.

In this same equation (tuition-plus-effort equals salary-plus-betterment), what do you think is the implication of an applicant who has paid especially high tuition?

PIECE OF MIND: MEDULLA OBLONGATA

Every signal between the brain and the body passes through the medulla oblongata, the piece of the brain stem connected to the spinal cord. It's also the home of many of our automatic functions: breathing, heart rate, vomiting, elimination, etc. In other words, the medulla oblongata takes care of our creature needs, on top of which a couple hundred million years of evolution have built the capacity for thought, language, and culture, making possible things like Socrates and the movie *Beverly Hills Chihuahua*.

The medulla oblongata may also be a counterintuitive component of the placebo effect— counterintuitive because the placebo effect has traditionally been attributed to higher areas of the brain capable of prediction, expectation, and evaluation (thought overrides pain). But researchers in Germany watched with high-tech gadgetry as placebos induced opioid release in the medulla oblongata. And rather than bouncing around the brain, these opioids traveled straight to the spinal cord, where they tamped down pain signals coming from the body before they even reached the brain.

PLACEBOS ARE GETTING STRONGER

Wired magazine reports that the placebo effect is getting stronger. Really: It seems our brain now responds more powerfully to false treatments than it did twenty or thirty years ago. This isn't just a nice bit of trivia; it has the potential to change the pharmaceutical business as we know it. In order for a new drug to be approved, it has to prove

its effectiveness. To do this, it has to beat placebos. And if it's getting harder and harder for drugs to beat placebos, then it's going to be harder to get new drugs to market.

Why is this happening?

One reason might be marketing: Drug companies are very good at raising our expectations, and with these high expectations of effectiveness, so too comes a high strength of the placebo effect. Also, many designer drugs are targeting more refined areas of the brain—no longer are we bludgeoning basic brain functions with the mallet of thorazine. Instead, drug companies are targeting higher-order disorders like social anxiety and various, precisely defined dysphorias. These dysfunctions live in the brain functions of expectation, evaluation, and prediction—the same functions that create the placebo effect.

MEERKATS, MACAQUES, MEN, AND THE HEALING EFFECTS OF FORGIVENESS

As viewers of the Discovery Channel know, meerkats' cuteness masks deep and tortured souls. And their homes, which initially appear to be rodent hippie communes, are in fact totalitarian states ruled by cruel alpha meerkat despots. These despots attack at their whim, after which there is no repair or forgiveness—if subordinates refuse to cooperate or otherwise retaliate, the despot will attack again. The best a victim can do is stay out of the aggressor's way.

Unlike meerkats, macaques and almost all primates follow aggression with reconciliation. In fact, friendly interactions between recent combatants are more likely than friendly interactions between two random macaques.

Humans, it seems, can choose to be meerkats or macaques—we can forgive or we can hold a grudge. One thing is clear: Forgiveness is good for you. The short-term effects of failing to immediately forgive the driver that cuts you off include increased blood pressure, heart rate, and galvanic skin response, the last implying that you get mad or scared . . . or sexually aroused (the increased ability of electricity to course through your skin prepares you for action of all sorts). Even after the short-term effects of anger have dissipated, forgiveness lowers your blood pressure and heart rate and is associated with a range of benefits including fewer medications, less alcohol use, better sleep, and even decreased lower-back pain. And people who forgive have better relationships: They accommodate, sacrifice, and cooperate, leading to lower divorce rates.

But it's difficult to punk the system: Forgiveness works best if you do it organically, rather than from feelings of obligation or in search of its health benefits. In other words, in order to reap the rewards of saying "That's OK," you have to mean it.

NEUROETHICS

Looking inside your head can tell us things about who you are and who you are likely to become. This is cool, but it's also pretty creepy in a Big-Brother-is-watching kinda way. Not to be fatalistic or technophobic or anything, but here are some ways the information previously hidden inside your head can be used against you:

• Criminal justice: Everyone deserves a second chance, right? What about the first-time sex offender who can be neurologically shown to have a predisposition for future crimes? For example, there's been research into the role of the brain protein monoamine oxidase A in criminality. Or, through the 1960s and '70s it was believed that men with XYY chromosomes were prone to increased violence (ac-

Wild Kingdom: Revenge!

Remember our fuzzy little feel-good macaques? Well, it turns out that forgiveness is only the rosy side of the postconflict spectrum. The other side of that spectrum is revenge. But if you're a wussy macaque who's been beat up by a dominant macaque, you certainly can't exact revenge on the dominant macaque directly.

Instead, you go after his family. In fact, if you're a Japanese macaque who's been beat up by the dominant male, there's a 29 percent chance that you'll attack a younger, weaker member of his family within the hour. And you'll do it right in front of him. That way, he'll know that beating you up results in injury to his family (hyenas do the same).

tually, they're prone to slightly decreased intelligence and have longer arrest records for petty crimes). Should criminals who are neurologically shown to have criminal minds be given longer sentences? More counseling? Shorter sentences because they can't be held accountable for their actions?

• Schools: The ACT has replaced the SAT with many college admissions boards. But what about the FCBS (Friggin' Cool Brain Scan)? Traditionally, school entrance exams measure ability with a side order of aptitude (mostly what we've shown we *can do*, with only a little about *what we're likely to be able to do*). What if a quick brain scan became a required component of the Harvard application? How smart are you *really*? And should your innate intelligence even matter if you've been able to compensate by study and hard work? What about neurological tests of personality? Should gifted and talented programs, private schools, and colleges be able to cherry pick students based on agreeableness?

• Business: Should insurers and employers be allowed to practice neuroscientific discrimination? Should employers be

allowed to monitor employees' attention during the workday (and automatically administer electrical shocks when workers' attention lags)? Should neoromarketers be allowed to monitor brain preferences while people shop (maybe similar to TV's Nielsen ratings)?

• Litigation: Lie detection and truth serum have been the holy grails of criminal trials since time immemorial. And what about jury selection? Should we discover the stereotypes in jurors' brains? Augmenting witnesses' memories of and confidence in the truth could aid trials too. Should juries in a personal-injury case be able to look inside a plaintiff's brain to see the extent of his chronic pain? Should juries know the neurology of a parent's competency in a custody case? Should juries know the neurological extent of a defendant's drug addiction?

I WOULD NEVER

Would you inflict pain for information, accept a government bailout for your inappropriate actions, or take financial advantage of another's ignorance?

Of course you wouldn't. But lots of other people would, right? It's a good thing the rest of the world can navigate by your moral compass.

Facebook Sexuality Prediction

Beware: The online information you'd prefer remained hidden isn't limited to spring break pictures and late-night blog comments. Students at MIT developed software that makes predictions based on Facebook profile data and friend lists. For example, even in men who preferred to keep their sexual orientation private, this software predicts with spooky accuracy who is likely to be gay. Perhaps insensitively, the students nicknamed their software Gaydar.

Researchers at Cornell University found that we're only slightly optimistic when predicting others' degree of morality but massively optimistic when predicting our own moral actions. When asked how many of their classmates would buy a daffodil at a campus-wide event supporting cancer research, 251 students said that 56 percent of all students would. In fact, 43 percent of students bought daffodils. But of these same students, 83 percent said they would, themselves, buy daffodils, almost doubly optimistic about their own behavior.

We overestimate our likelihood of voting and our willingness to help strangers. That is, unless we have direct experience with the problem. For example, we're much better at predicting our own use of shady accounting practices if we've ever had to put a happy face on a failing business. (To know a man, walk a day with his calculator.)

In light of our shared moral failings, think about the desire to fire all immoral politicians and replace them with moral ones. This would cleanse the political system of corruption, right?

Read the statements below and use a pencil to score each question's accuracy in describing your thoughts or behaviors, with one being "very inaccurate" and five being "very accurate." Flip to the back of the book for interpretation.

1. I am told that I'm down to earth.

2. I can be trusted to keep my promises.

3. I am true to my own values.

4. I feel like an imposter.

5. I am told by friends that they do not really know who I am.

6. I keep my promises.

7. I lie to get myself out of trouble.

8. I believe that honesty is the basis for trust.

9. I take pride in not exaggerating who or what I am.

10. I am hard to understand.

11. I like to exaggerate my troubles.

Eye Hack: Blivets

The seeming simplicity of the Penrose triangle and devil's tuning fork makes the mental anguish they cause that much more acute. Impossible shapes like these are called *blivets*. The word is also used to describe anything that once unpacked can't be returned to its box.

Will and Grace

Are you honest or are you a liar? A Harvard neuroimaging study showed that you're wired to be one or the other. The study watched subjects' brains as they were presented with the opportunity to win money through lying. When honest people told the truth, their brains were at peace. When dishonest people lied, the control centers of their brains crackled to overwrite the truth with a lie. And here's the cool part: Even when dishonest people happened to tell the truth, researchers watched their brains actively override the temptation to lie.

And so there is neurological support for both the "Will" and "Grace" theories of truth-telling: some people simply tell the truth (Grace) and some actively override the temptation to lie (Will).

MEMORIZATION 101

Imagine you're learning Spanish. You might have a list of English words and their Spanish equivalents and there's naught to do but sit down and memorize it.

Here's the thing: You'll memorize the list better if you look at the English alone then check the Spanish if needed, than if you look at both English and Spanish at the same time.

This is called the testing effect: Your memory is enhanced by forcing it to recall things, rather than simply seeing or hearing them. In other words, you can read the English/Spanish list all you want, but it's much better to read the English and try to recall the Spanish before looking at the answer.

Likewise, it's good to take notes during Spanish class, but it's better to take notes *after* class. By forcing your memory to reproduce the lecture, you reinforce your memory of it. (That is, unless taking notes *during* class is the only way you'll stay awake.)

But beware the catch: If you blow it and when looking at the English word "peaches" incorrectly recall the word *"desnudos"* instead of *"duraznos,"* you'll have a difficult time retraining your mind to correctly ask for peaches instead of naked men.

DOES SUBLIMINAL ADVERTISING WORK?

Morality is the weakness of the brain.

—Arthur Rimbaud

When you play Zeppelin's "Stairway to Heaven" backward, can you actually hear the words "oh here's to my sweet Satan"? When James Vicary flashed the words "Drink Coca-Cola" and "Hungry? Eat Popcorn!" did food sales at a New Jersey movie theater increase by over 50 percent? Did a one-frame flash of "Buy Bonds" in the 1943 film classic *The Wise Quacking Duck* win the war for Allied troops?

In all cases, the answer is no.

Despite the hubbub, including the FCC's 1974 ban on subliminal advertising, the technique's rarely been shown to be effective. In fact, James Vicary admitted that he faked his famous experiments that started the buzz in the first place (though his stunt *did* get the words Coca-Cola a substantial burst of free airtime).

That said, recent studies have found subliminal advertising to be somewhat—but only somewhat—effective, and in interesting ways. First, there's a major catch: customers have to already be in the mood. They have to be thirsty in order for the subliminal signal "Lipton Ice" to make them buy more tea; they have to be tired before subliminal priming will make them eat more "attention" pills. And, interestingly, the effect easily strays: Subjects primed with the word "beef" showed no preference for steak over chicken, but proved to be hungrier in general.

The verdict: Perhaps with refinement, subliminal advertising could become a tool of indescribable evil, but in it's current state—meh. . . .

Self-Test:
Quick Memory Check

1. Remember this name and address:

   John Doe
   6285 Central Street
   Boston, MA

2. Remember these words: popcorn, horse, Frisbee

3. What was the main course of your dinner the past two nights?

4. What did you wear yesterday and the day before?

5. List the past five United States presidents.

6. List four state capitals.

7. List four kinds of birds.

8. List four teachers you had in school.

9. Who are the current vice president, secretary of state, and speaker of the house?

10. Write down the three words you were asked to remember at the beginning of the quiz.

11. Write down the name and address you were asked to remember at the beginning of the quiz.

Scoring:

Give yourself 1 point for each piece of information you remembered (count each address line as a point).

If you scored:

27–30   Your mind is a steel trap.

20–26   Yeah, whatever.

13–19   Duh, whatever.

0–12   Consider a professional evaluation.

Logic of Illogic: K Words

Do you think there are more words in the English language that start with K, or more words in which K is the third letter?

Seriously, think about it: kitten . . .
kangaroo . . .
acknowledge . . .
ankylosaur . . .

Did you choose *starts with K*? If you did, you're not alone. Far more people pick *starts with* than *third letter*.

In fact, there are about three times as many English words with a K in the third position than in the first. But because sticking a K at the beginning of a word gives us a first sound to work from, it's easier to think of words that start with K. This is a clear example of decision-making led by an availability heuristic: These words that start with K pop to mind and based on this availability we assume they're more prevalent.

The same availability heuristic affects our fear of flying (crashes are spectacular and pop quickly to mind despite flying's relative overall safety) and our decision to underinvest in the stock market (again, spectacular crashes mask greater overall safety).

GENIUS TESTER #9: THE PSYCHOLOGY OF GETTING SUCKERED

In a totally sweet *New York Times* article of this title, John Tierney discusses a probability experiment conducted by professors Craig Fox and Jonathan Levav.

Here's how it works.

One of the profs shuffles five cards, one of which is an ace, and then deals two cards to a participant and keeps three for himself. All cards are facedown. No peeking. If the participant's hand happens to have the ace, he earns $1.

Easy, right?

Here's the first twist: The prof peeks at his own cards and then offers the participant the chance to switch hands. Duh. Most of the participants see that the odds of getting an ace are 3 to 5 for switching and 2 to 5 for keeping their own hand, and so most of them choose to switch.

Now, what do you think happened when the good professor told a second group of participants that he would look at his cards, turn up two cards that are not the ace, and then offer them a chance to switch hands?

Check the answer. It's as good as the puzzle.

Psy-Op: Pick a Number, Any Number

For this trick to work, you gotta do it like you mean it. Do the math in your head as quickly as you can. Then flip to the back for the answer. Ready? Go!!

What is:

- 6–2?

- 8–4?

- 12–8?

- 16–12?

Now quickly pick a number between 12 and 5!

WILD KINGDOM: PIGEON AFICIONADO

When one imagines a pigeon, one doesn't necessarily think *lover of art*. But it's true that many pigeons live in cities and much art is produced and exhibited in cities. Maybe this explains the work of Japanese researchers who, in 1995, found that pigeons could distinguish between works of Monet and Picasso, and could correctly label paintings they'd never seen before as works of one artist or the other. The pigeons also lumped Cézanne and Renoir with Monet, and Braque and Matisse with Picasso. (OK, full disclosure: the researchers *taught* the pigeons the Monet/Picasso distinction, but still, it's pretty cool that the pigeons then extended these categories to other artists.)

Interestingly, turning a Monet upside down threw off the art-loving pigeons. Turning a Picasso upside down did not.

NEURAL DARWINISM

Our brain is a huge highway system of neurons, with about one quadrillion (10^{15}) synapses where roads cross. Like cars on a map, information can flow through this system many ways. But, again like roads, there's always one way that's fastest. How does information choose the fastest way?

The answer is that the brain learns to efficiently route information through trial and error. And in a process very similar to natural selection, the pathways that are proven to work survive and those that don't are pruned from the system.

Here's how it works:

First, early in our prenatal development, our brain lays neural pavement, including freeways, arterial roads, roundabouts, and culs-de-sac. Now, in the absence of GPS and Google Earth, the only thing to do is drive the roads blindly, which we do through infancy. Every time a baby receives input, many cars travel many roads, some choosing efficient paths and many hitting roundabouts and roadblocks.

Every time information travels a route, it trains the synapses along this route to fire slightly faster, like optimizing the traffic lights at crossroads. And so the roads that correctly transmit the information gain efficiency. Eventually the proven routes become significantly faster than the others and the inefficient routes are closed off entirely.

Now when a stimulus enters the system, it knows exactly where to go and follows the same, efficient route every time.

STRETCHING PHANTOM LIMB CRAMPS

Dr. Ramachandran's patient complained of a terrible arm cramp. It had been cramped, said the patient, for about ten years. If only he could move the arm, he thought the cramp would go away. The problem was, the man was no longer in possession of the arm, and thus couldn't move it. It had been amputated about ten years ago.

Here's Dr. Ramachandran's solution:

He asked the man to hold a mirror perpendicular to his midline and then twist it until the mirror showed his intact arm in the place of the missing arm. As you might know from trying

Brain Map

Never fear, inefficient drivers, soon there will be a comprehensive map showing not only the pathways of the brain, but also which genes are responsible for paving the roads (and which are to blame for faulty paving). The Allen Institute for Brain Science in Seattle is mapping every gene responsible for the growth of the brain. Like the Human Genome Project, the map will allow biomedical researchers to link defects with genes, leading to new forms of diagnosis and treatment.

to shave a missed hair or from interlacing your fingers and trying to lift the third finger on your right hand, the mind's perspective is easily tricked by mirrors.

Such was the case with Dr. Ramachandran's patient.

The patient wiggled his intact arm, while tricking his mind into seeing it as the phantom limb. Now that he was able to "move" this phantom limb, the cramp went away.

SHEEPLE

Imagine two restaurants of comparable quality. Along comes the evening's first customer, who has to choose between these two restaurants. He flips a coin and

Psy-Op: Phantom Nose

Cross your fingers. Now stroke the tip of your nose in the notch of your crossed fingers, such that the tips of both crossed fingers touch it. Do you feel the disembodied second nose? If you do, it's because the opposite sides of our first and second fingers are used to feeling things separated by space. By crossing your fingers, you use one object (your nose) to impersonate the sensation usually created by two objects.

picks restaurant A. Now imagine the next customer. Confronted with the same choice, she has the same information plus she sees the first customer sitting in the window of restaurant A. What does she do?

You can see where this is going.

But at this point, restaurant B still has hope—how much does the second customer trust the first customer's choice? Well, is he attractive? Does he smoke? How's he dressed? What's his posture? The more the second person identifies with the first, the more she trusts his choice.

Once the second customer chooses restaurant A too, it starts to solidify a consensus. The third customer would have to buck a significant trend, voting against two people, in order to choose restaurant B.

Soon, you can imagine a line out the door of restaurant A, while restaurant B sits empty—despite the restaurants' similar quality.

While this example is admittedly simplified—at a certain point people choose restaurant B specifically because too many others are in A—the pull of the sheeple effect is nonetheless strong and can at times result in baaaad choices (and worse jokes . . .).

GAME THEORY MAKE BRAIN BIG: DINER'S DILEMMA

You go out to eat with a group and agree to split the check evenly at the end. There are only two things on the menu, one expensive and one cheap. If you were alone, you'd order the cheap one, because the expensive one isn't *that much* better. But with the extra cost split across the group, you just might order the expensive item.

What do you do?

WILD KINGDOM: ANALYTIC ANTS

Imagine you're buying a house and you've narrowed the decision to two choices. One day, you're ready to slap a down payment on house A and the next day you vacillate—with some work, wouldn't house B's outbuilding make a great office?

This is irrational.

The houses haven't changed, and so if you were acting rationally, your brain would simply sum up which house is best for you and you'd buy it. There is a right answer and the right answer is fixed. There's no rational reason for waffling.

Ants don't. This is because ants are more rational than you.

In fact, individual ants are no better than you when choosing between two generally comparable options, but a colony's power of collective decision-making ensures that as a whole, the colony makes the best choice. Researchers showed this by presenting a colony of ants with the choice of two generally comparable nest sites. Each site had plusses and minuses—one was slightly closer to food, while the other was in slightly preferable soil, etc.

Here's what happened:

Ants found the two sites. And when an individual found a site, it determined whether the site was habitable. If it was habitable, the ant simply started hauling in its gear—food, eggs, that treadmill it hadn't touched in a year but would certainly use to qualify for the Boston Marathon, etc. And here's the trick: The better the site, the higher the percentage of ants that found it habitable. So over time, more ants voted for the better site. More votes moved more resources and soon the better site was better stocked, and being better stocked made it obviously more habitable. The snowball rolled and this site became the de facto choice of the group as a whole.

Here's the cool thing: Most people admit that an individual ant is less complex than an individual human. But as we've seen, there are situations in which ants make better decisions. How do they do it? Instead of depending on one complex brain, ants have off-loaded decision making from the individual into the collective mainframe. They have a "decentralized" decision mechanism. And so, many simple ants acting in their own simple ways combine to create complex decisions.

Think about this in terms of artificial intelligence: It's very difficult to model the human brain. It's just too complex. But it's not out of the question to model ant behavior—they act in certain defined ways every time. And from a colony of simple ant-bots, one could potentially generate emergent behavior as powerful as the decisions of the human brain.

Logic of Illogic: Fruit Bag

Imagine a bag of apples, oranges, and pears. There are 30 pieces of fruit, exactly 10 of which are apples. You don't know how the remaining 20 fruits are split. There could be 20 oranges, or 20 pears, or anything in between. If you name a fruit and then pick it blindly on the first try, you earn $100. Which fruit do you pick? (Assume they're all the same size, texture, etc., so that there's no way to cheat by feeling around in the bag.)

If you're like most people you "go with what you know," that is, you try to pick an apple. After all, you know there are 10 apples and there may not be any oranges.

Then again, there may be 20 oranges.

In fact, there's no right choice: Picking an apple, an orange, or a pear is equally likely. (Because the probability of orange or pear is split across 0–20, the average probability is 10, just like the apples.)

But the brain dislikes ambiguity. The unknown scares us. We'd much rather go with the known, even if it's equal to or less than the unknown.

Eye Hack: Jastrow Illusion

If figure A were placed on top of figure B, what percentage of figure B's area would remain uncovered?

The answer is exactly 0 percent.

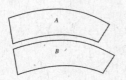

In 1848, Phineas Gage was the foreman of a prison work gang that was blasting the path for a railroad bed in Vermont. After the crew drilled blast holes, it was Gage's job to add gunpowder and tamp it down, which he did with a thirteen-pound, nearly four-foot-long iron spike. On September 13 of that year, Gage tamped a little too hard.

The gunpowder exploded, blasting the tamping rod back toward Gage. According to the accident report, "the iron entered on the side of his face, shattering the upper jaw, and passing back of the left eye, and out at the top of the head," from whence the spike continued, landing nearly eighty feet away.

Gage remained conscious,

and after sitting upright during the mile-long cart ride into town, he regaled a gathered crowd with the story of his injury. The first physician on the scene recalled that Gage "got up and vomited; the effort of vomiting pressed out about half a teacupful of the brain, which fell upon the floor."

Amazingly, despite almost completely ineffectual treatment and subsequent brain infection, Gage recovered.

But while Gage's physical recovery was total, Dr. John Harlow describes changes in Gage's personality: Before the accident, Gage was hardworking, responsible, "a great favorite" with the men in his charge, and regarded by his employers as "the most efficient and capable foreman in their employ." After the accident, Harlow writes that, "The equilibrium or balance, so to speak, between his intellectual faculties and animal propensities, seems to have been destroyed."

Gage became impulsive and irrational. Harlow wrote, "In this regard his mind was radically changed, so decidedly that his friends and acquaintances said he was no longer Gage."

This raises the existential question of *what is Gage?* Is he, or are we, defined by our thoughts and actions, or is there an inviolable piece of Gage—

his soul, perhaps—that was unchanged by the accident?

You can find a wonderful, if graphic, animation of Gage's injury in a post by "Mo" by Googling "Gage neurophilosophy."

Eye Hack: Ebbinghaus Illusion

The center circles are exactly the same size. Really, they are.

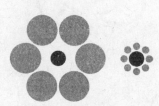

IS LAUGHTER THE BEST MEDICINE?

Laughter as the best medicine has been folk wisdom since time immemorial, but until Norman Cousins it wasn't the subject of much scholarly debate. Cousins was the writer and editor of the *Saturday Review* in the 1970s, when he was diagnosed with an autoimmune disease. Medical literature was pretty clear that stress made the disease worse, so, Cousins reasoned, shouldn't less stress make it better? He prescribed himself a steady diet of *Candid Camera* episodes and started laughing as much as he could. The disease went into remission. Cousins published his experiences in the *New England Journal of Medicine,* spawning academic research in the new field of whole-person care.

That people who laugh more are in better health is undisputable: They sleep better, have lower blood pressure, and are sick less, and a study of diabetics who attended a boring lecture one night and watched a comedy the next found lower blood-sugar levels after the comedy.

But which is the chicken and which is the egg? Does laughter make you healthier, or do healthier people simply have more to laugh about? It's extremely difficult to disentangle laughter from existing personality. It's also unclear whether laughter, specifically, is good medicine or whether its supposed health effects are simply those of release, similar to exercise or a good scream.

Humor is by far the most significant activity of the human brain.

—Edward de Bono

THE IMPACT OF TRAGEDY

The attention we give to (or withhold from) tragedies has

little to do with numbers: Many hundreds can die in a cholera outbreak in Zimbabwe or hundreds of thousands in an earthquake in China and it receives nowhere near the press and public outrage as nearly 200 killed in terrorist attacks in Mumbai. (This isn't meant to diminish the tragedy of Mumbai, only to act as comparison.)

Still, we can imagine the evolutionary logic of this: Our mind quickly jumps to the cause of a disaster, evaluating it for relevance to our own survival. Once we've "solved the crime" of culpability, it's as if the case is closed—we know what to be wary of and our brains can move on. Thus, because we understand the causes and risks of natural disasters (and may take a similar point of view about car bombings in areas in which they've become commonplace), the tragedies that grab our attention are those that are unexpected, and that have causes and motivations we struggle to explain. The Mumbai gun attacks make everyone nervous because, well, we wonder if it could happen here, to us.

Intention matters, too. Shankar Vedantam points out in an article for the *Washington Post* that the person who tries to kill a child and fails is seen as worse

Bad Poetry Aids in Recovery

It's no surprise that writing about emotional turmoil helps the brain process it. But it turns out that the best therapeutic writing is bad poetry. Unlike good poetry, bad poetry is devoid of vivid description, which could itself trigger stress. From phobias to daily distresses to past traumas, writing detached verse or sappy song lyrics can provide emotional regulation.

than the drunk driver who kills a child in an accident.

Most of the time, assigning increased blame to people with bad intentions is logical: People who intend harm generally *do* the most harm. But, as Vedantam points out, punishment is often influenced by results as well as intention. The person who stabs and kills a person is punished much differently than the person who stabs with the intention to kill, but whose victim survives.

Is the crime any different?

Does the terrorist who kills two people in a conventional bombing deserve harsher punishment than the terrorist whose plot to set off a nuclear bomb is foiled by James Bond as the bomb ticks toward zero?

So, struggling to understand a tragedy's cause, finding that this cause is malicious, and seeing extreme results from this intention all increase our outrage. And when all three align, as in the case of successful terrorism, our outrage is extreme and so too can be our response.

iDread

Metrophobia: fear of poetry.

To most of us, this feels *right*. More difficult is logically evaluating when our "extreme" response exceeds the bounds of reason and justice.

FRUIT VS. VEGGIE PERSONALITY SMACKDOWN

Which do you prefer: fruits or vegetables? Imagine: a cold slice of watermelon on a hot day versus perfectly grilled veggie skewers.

Your choice is telling. Fruit people are very different from vegetable people. Vegetable people drink more wine, use more spice, and spend more time experimenting in the kitchen. Fruit people eat more candy and desserts, cook more familiar meals, and entertain fewer guests.

DEFLECTING INCOMING BLOOPERS

Who hasn't spilled a cup of coffee or stubbed a toe or miscalculated the approach trajectory of a hundred-thousand-pound airliner? We don't mean to do these things. They just happen in that millisecond when we take our minds off what we're doing.

And it turns out that in the millisecond before our minds wander, our brain does something funny: The occipital lobe and the sensorimotor cortex light up. This same pattern occurs when we close our eyes—without visual information to process, we turn inward for stimulus.

Now that we've mapped the pattern of inattention, we could (theoretically, according to researchers at the University of California–Davis) take corrective action *before the blunder occurs.* Perhaps air traffic controllers could wear helmets that monitor brain activity and deliver an electrical shock when attention lags?

Imagine a classroom full of kids with these helmets. In kids with ADHD or others prone to wandering minds, the electrical shocks could be especially strong. Wouldn't this be a brave new world?

Horror Film PTSD

Are you traumatized by terror flicks? Maybe more than you know. Scary movies actually create a light version of post-traumatic stress disorder. This is what causes bad dreams and irrational fears of kids riding Big Wheels in hotel hallways.

And by exploring how people stop these dreams and fears, researchers are learning how we might combat more serious PTSD. For instance, researchers find that talking about a horror movie afterward reduces the occurrence of bad dreams.

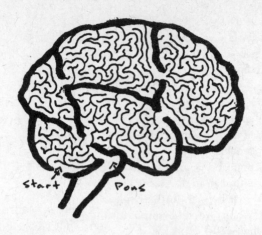

Start   Pons

PIECE OF MIND: PONS

The pons is your *dirty mind*—the home of arousal—and sits like a tennis ball atop your brain stem. It's also the conduit for sensory information traveling between the cerebellum and the cerebrum, and is responsible for flipping the switch to REM sleep. Partly because of its role in sleep, many also think the pons is where dreams are made. Certainly, during REM sleep, it spews a neurotransmitter that lights various dream centers, but whether it does this of its own accord or whether the pons is a pawn to higher regions of the brain is still up for debate.

ALGEBRAIC EIGHT-BALL: MEN, WHAT'S YOUR SEX APPEAL?

• T = If you can see your toes while standing, enter zero. If not, enter the inches of reduced belt size needed to restore podiatric vision.

• H_H = Percentage of scalp showing through hair.

• H_B = Percentage of body below neck showing through hair.

• M = Go to a park. Smile at ten mothers. How many smile back? Subtract from this the number of children who cry.

- O_+ = How many of the following do you have or have you had: a gym membership, a cat or dog, silk boxer shorts, a motorcycle, shoes that cost more than 100 bucks, sex in the past month, massage oil and/or bubble bath.

- O_- = How many of the following do you have: snake or rat, underwear with holes, a video-game machine, Velcro shoes, a condom past its expiration date, any personalized or joke beer paraphernalia, your mother's phone number on speed dial.

- S_S = Your shoe size.

- X = Subtract five if you actually solved this equation.

$$25\left(\sqrt{\frac{H_B}{H_H + 25}}\right)\left(\frac{M + O_+ + S_S + 25}{T + O_- + 25}\right) - X = S_{exAppeal}$$

INTERPRETATION OF RESULTS

90–100	Filet mignon
70–89	Porterhouse
40–69	Sirloin
10–39	Ground round
0–9	Jerky

Windows 2000 already contains features such as the human discipline component, where the PC can send an electric shock through the keyboard if the human does something that does not please Windows.

—Widely misattributed to Bill Gates

Psy-Op: Veggie Math

For this trick to work, you gotta do it like you mean it. Start at the top and do the math in your head as quickly as possible. Then follow the instructions. Ready? Go!!

What is:

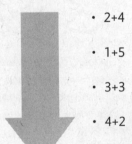

- 2+4

- 1+5

- 3+3

- 4+2

- 5+1

Now think of a vegetable! Quick!! Flip to the answers section at the back.

ABNORMAL PSYCH: AHAD ISRAFIL

Fourteen-year-old Ahad Israfil was at work when his employer knocked a shotgun off a counter and accidentally blew off half of Israfil's head. The EMTs on the scene were surprised that Israfil survived the trip to the hospital. Surgeons were flabbergasted when, after a five-hour operation, Israfil regained consciousness and tried to speak.

In fact, with literally half his brain missing, Israfil recovered enough to graduate with honors from his local university. You can find video of Israfil online.

THE BURDEN OF CONVENTIONAL THINKING

John robbed a bank. Now he's serving ten years. Writing in the *New Yorker*, Malcolm Gladwell points out that in the previous sentences, our brain fills in the information "John was apprehended, tried, and convicted." Computers don't do this. In fact, duplicating this ability to sift through huge stores of background knowledge and seamlessly plug story-line gaps is one of the major challenges of artificial intelligence.

But it also means that computers can sometimes think outside the box created by human expectations.

This was the case, Gladwell writes, when Stanford computer scientist Doug Lenat unleashed his program Eurisko on the Traveller Trillion Credit Squadron competition. In this competition, players are given hypothetical trillion dollar budgets, which they use to design navies. Then the navies battle mano a mano, with the winner advancing to the next round. Being human, we know that the best navies include a mix of cruisers, destroyers, carriers, etc., all strategically deployed and utilized. But Lenat's program Eurisko didn't know this. Instead, it read the rules of the game and designed the best strategy: a swarm of miniscule PT boats with big guns, no movement, and no defense whatsoever.

Eurisko cleaned up.

The next year, the competition changed the requirements, adding a minimum movement requirement. Eurisko used the same strategy, with exactly the minimum required movement. When a ship was damaged so that it

Math Outsmarts Brains

The Bay of Biscay is off the west coast of France, south of the English Channel. During World War II, Royal Air Force patrols frequently spotted enemy submarines there. Certainly it was best to heavily patrol this area where the most submarines were found. Right?

It turned out that submarines were found here due to *patrol* density, not submarine density, and that patrol *efficiency* was higher in other areas. When RAF commanders sent patrols elsewhere, efficiency was increased and fewer planes were able to find more submarines. The field of Operations Research was born.

brought Eurisko's navy below the required movement minimum, Eurisko sank its own slowed ship.

Eye Hack: AI Necker

The Necker cube (left) has been used to test visual recognition software: Can a computer figure out which face points out? Once a computer arrives at the conclusion, can it switch its opinion like the human mind? The impossible cube on the right just hurts our minds.

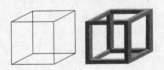

Eurisko cleaned up.

The competition organizers asked that Lenat refrain from entering the competition a third time.

It's certainly cool to think about how computers show us the shackles of our conventional thinking. But we needn't even look as far as the microchip for this. In fact, there are many human brains that don't play by the rules. We label these brains ADHD or dyslexic or autistic. Should we medicate these brains back onto the bell curve, or does humanity need this novel thinking to help us innovate? Does society's need for innovative thinkers outweigh the needs and rights of individuals living with challenging brains, who could live easier lives with medication? This certainly isn't the first book to ask these questions.

GAME THEORY MAKE BRAIN BIG: PEACE/WAR

Players represent countries. In each round, countries choose peace or war (one, two, three, shoot!).

Here's the payoff:

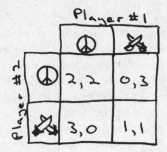

This means that if both shoot "peace," both earn two points; if both shoot war, both earn one point; if one shoots war and the other peace, the aggressor earns three points and the victim earns zero.

Now imagine that many countries are playing at the same time. What's the best strategy?

I was taught that the human brain was the crowning glory of evolution so far, but I think it's a very poor scheme for survival.

—Kurt Vonnegut, Jr.

TIME TRAVEL: SCIENCE, NOT SCIENCE FICTION

Right now, you can travel to the past or experience the future— all from the comfort of your own brain. Just imagine it. Really, that's all you have to do: Imagine the past or future and there you are.

This is true of more than just pictures. When our mind time-travels forward or back, we ex-perience muted versions of the emotions associated with the scene. We don't just remember the past, we relive it; and we don't simply imagine the future, we experience the likely emotional impacts of our decisions.

But why? Why are we forced to cringe and blush even now when remembering hitting a parked car while waving to our first real girlfriend after dropping her off at the passenger terminal of the Bainbridge Island ferry? Why do our knees shake and our usually robust constitutions turn to banana jelly when we imagine falling from a rock climb?

It turns out, as you might imagine, that connecting emotion with events in memory (mental time travel) adds weight to events. The more emotionally charged a memory, the more influential it is in determining our future choices.

As a practical consequence, mental time travel squeezes our range of choices toward the center. Remembering embarrassment, we refrain from the further hitting of parked cars; imagining fear, we don't put ourselves in the dangerous situation that would create it (or, we do, but we're aware of the consequences). We become more careful, less impulsive. The results of our choices become less extreme.

Mental time travel allows us to predict the social as well as physical results of our actions—we know that if we post mean comebacks on our Facebook friends' walls (even when they're wrong), we'll be excommunicated from the group. We know that it's a good idea to compliment a friend's ugly baby.

Humans are social, and the mental time travel of linking emotion with memories and using them to live in the future allows us to remain so.

The Age of Time Travel

An Australian study found that very few three-year-olds but most four-year-olds could describe two things they did yesterday and predict two things they would do tomorrow (as well as two things they *didn't* do yesterday and two things they *wouldn't* do tomorrow). It seems our fourth birthday is our passport for time travel.

ACTIVE FORGETTING: THE MENTAL BOXES OF SUPPRESSION AND REPRESSION

As you read this, don't think about a white bear. Stop! Seriously, don't think about it.

You might as well admit it: You need help.

Genius Tester #10: Time Travel

Look at this clock:

How would the hands look if the following were done?

1. The clock was sent back in time five minutes.

2. The clock itself stopped in time.

3. The clock was sent five minutes ahead in time.

Here are two strategies you might try. First, increase your cognitive load: Concentrate on everything around you *except* the bear. This is like having a picnic and concentrating on the food, the weather, your company, and the sounds of birds to the exclusion of the fast-approaching polar bear.

Or you can try picking one thing to concentrate on instead

of the bear. Dr. Daniel M. Wegner, a leading researcher in the field of thought suppression, has asked subjects to think about a red Volkswagen. At the picnic, this is like parking the Volkswagen so that it blocks your view of the bear.

Unfortunately, neither method works. They're only temporary fixes, allowing you to put aside distressing thoughts until you can later deal with them (it's unclear if using a blue Volkswagen or perhaps a Buick might be more successful).

And deal with them you must. The bear will not be stopped by active ignoring or by blocking. It's coming to your picnic whether you like it or not. In fact, suppressing this thought only increases its power (David Carradine on the show *Kung Fu:* "To suppress a truth is to give it force beyond endurance"). This is called the rebound effect—people who suppress unwanted thoughts end up having the thought *more frequently* than people who deal with the unwanted thought as it occurs. Also, we tend to link our suppression mechanisms with the unwanted thought—now, forevermore, when you picnic or see red Volkswagens, you'll expect the arrival of the damned bear.

This is a vicious cycle: The bear pokes through your blanket of suppression, prompting you to focus more energy on suppression, and soon you find yourself scrubbing the bathroom tile grout at three in the morning, trying to cleanse your mind of ursine thoughts. This is obsessive-compulsive disorder—your attempts at further suppression become all-consuming in a process similar to a methamphetamine user needing ever increasing amounts of the drug to achieve the same effect.

Let's say it again, simply: suppression doesn't work.

So give up. Think about the bear. No kidding, take a couple seconds. There, doesn't that feel better? Now you can picnic in peace (albeit with the bear sitting on your checkered tablecloth eating chicken salad).

But what if the bear (this unwanted thought) were so heinous that thinking about it posed a major risk to your being? What if the bear, if allowed to your picnic, would eat you whole?

This is a different beast entirely, one over which you have no conscious control. The only answer here is *repression,* when your subconscious takes over to save you from egregious psychic harm. Your mind's powers of repression can stuff that bear into a cage so dark and so deep within your psyche that you might never remember having seen it at all. This is what Oprah did with her memories of child abuse.

But just because the thought itself is unable to poke through a repression blanket doesn't mean that it's gone completely. Somewhere, deep inside you, the bear lives. You now own the damn bear. And you have to feed it.

Symptoms of repression can be many and far-reaching, ranging from thought and behavior quirks to physical pain. And remember—the source of these symptoms is now hidden beneath layers and layers of heavy blankets. Enter many thousands of dollars of psychotherapy.

The moral of this bear story is, if at all possible, to deal with bears at your picnic—you'd rather get a couple scratches right away while shooing the bear from your blanket than end up caging the bear inside yourself long-term.

Zen Mind

Tanzan and Ekido met a lovely girl who was unable to cross a muddy road.

"Come on, girl," said Tanzan at once. Lifting her in his arms, he carried her over the mud.

Ekido did not speak again until that night when they reached a lodging temple. "We monks don't go near females," he told Tanzan, "especially not young and lovely ones. It is dangerous. Why did you do that?"

"I left the girl there," said Tanzan. "Are you still carrying her?"

A man should keep his little brain attic stocked with all the furniture that he is likely to use, and the rest he can put away in the lumber-room of his library, where he can get it if he wants it.

—Sir Arthur Conan Doyle

IGNORING IS EXHAUSTING

It's not that you switch off the portion of your brain that hears the drip, drip, drip of a leaky faucet while you're trying to read a book. It's that you use prefrontal brainpower to actively *block* the sound, leaving less brainpower for your book.

In fact, the mechanics of suppressing any thought—be it a leaky faucet or a traumatic memory—are almost exactly those of checking the swing of a bat: You exert executive control to override impulse. And have you seen players' faces when they try to hold up? It takes effort. And like steroidal ballplayers, people with stronger prefrontal cortexes are better at suppressing unwanted memories.

Here's the cool part: Suppressing builds strength, at least in the case of the specific unwanted memory. Once you've suppressed a memory, your brain is trained to do so with less effort next time.

EXERCISE MAKES YOU SMART

Exercise makes your muscles stronger. Why not your brain, too? You might not be surprised to learn that exercise tends to result in overall mood elevation and that a better mood equals cleaner thinking, but exercise goes far past feelings, actually affecting the shape of the brain itself— exercise promotes neuron growth, helps the brain recover from injury, and turns on genes that promote brain plasticity. In other words, exercise makes your brain buff on a very basic level.

But don't overdo it.

Overly strenuous, lengthy, or discontinuous bouts of exercise *decrease* cognition and memory. Perhaps this lends support to dumb jock theory (DJT).

DO CROSS-WORDS KEEP THE BRAIN YOUNG?

Working memory is your brain's temporary storage. It's where information's briefly held before it's passed into the brain for deeper storage, and where memory sits when recalled from the brain for use. It also releases unneeded information to the great circular file of forgetting. As its name implies, working memory is where we *work*—it holds the beginnings of sentences long enough for you to extract meaning from them at the end.

It also depends on dopamine synapses. It's at these junctions that information passes into and out of working memory. And so the more dopamine receptors you have (places where dopa-

> Golfers instructed to avoid a specific mistake, like overshooting, do it more often when under pressure. Soccer players told to shoot a penalty kick anywhere but at a certain spot of the net, like the lower right corner, look at that spot more often than any other.
>
> —Benedict Carey,
> *New York Times*

mine synapses can attach), the better your working memory.

And using your working memory to do crosswords actually creates more dopamine receptors in areas of the brain relevant to working memory. In other words, doing the crossword sculpts the biology of your brain for better recall.

Eye Hack:
Fraser Spiral

About the Fraser spiral: it's not a spiral. It's a series of concentric circles.

I SHOP, THERE-
FORE I AM

It's no secret that the brands you ally yourself with express who you are. If you watch *Ghost-busters*, drive a Subaru with a roof rack, listen to the Beatles and world-music mixes, drink dark coffee and microbrews, and read *The Hobbit* and *Surely You're Joking, Mr. Feynman!*, we have a fairly accurate picture of your personality.

In fact, this is what Facebook does when it asks and then displays your brand preferences. Because we're used to being lied to online—*You've won 50 million pounds in the Irish national lottery!*—instead of *telling* on Facebook, we *show*. To sociologists, this is *implicit* construction of personality rather than *explicit*. We imply who we are by showing what we like.

But is our use of brands to express our identity a one-way street? Instead, is it possible for brands not just to demonstrate, but to *create* our identity?

Sociologists take the phrase "I shop, therefore I am" seriously. If you use brands to display your identity, then shopping, they say, allows us to preview different identities—just as we try on different pairs of jeans, we try on different selves. And thus finding the right pair of jeans is a form of self-discovery. And with this discovery complete, you find that you are a Gap person or an Abercrombie person (a subtle but important distinction, I'm told). And once you go Gap, you don't

Genius Tester #11:
The Monty Hall Problem

Here's the puzzle as presented in *Parade* magazine and popularized in the movie *Good Will Hunting*:

Suppose you're on a game show, and you're given the choice of three doors: Behind one door is a car; behind the others, goats. You pick a door, say number one, and the host, who knows what's behind the doors, opens another door, say number three, which has a goat. He then says to you, "Do you want to pick door number two?" Is it to your advantage to switch your choice?

Check the solution. It's as good as the puzzle.

go back—allying yourself with brands affects how others see you, which in turn affects how you see yourself, which affects who you are on a very basic level.

So beware what you wear—your clothes might be wearing you.

input into a form recognizable by the cerebral cortex. Damage to the thalamus can result in creepy tactile misinformation. And because it's also involved in sleep and wakefulness, damage can also result in coma.

PIECE OF MIND: THALAMUS

The thalamus is actually two kidney-shaped thalami (not to be confused with the longer, tastier "salami"), which sit low in the brain. It's a region of many functions but primarily acts as a relay station, processing sensory

BIOLOGICAL BASIS OF ROSE-COLORED GLASSES

Remember the good old days of soda parlors, high school pep rallies, Buddy Holly, and nonsteroidal baseball? Everything used to be better, right?

This nostalgia exists partially

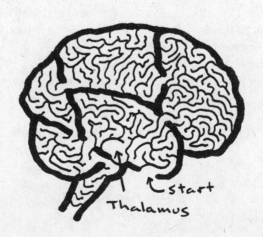

because aging brains jettison bad memories.

Researchers showed participants a series of images and asked them to rate the images on a pleasantness scale. Later, they asked the participants to recall these images. Older participants remembered fewer unpleasant images than younger participants.

Here's how it works in the brain:

Brain scans showed that when older participants were shown unpleasant images, the amygdala (emotion) had less interaction with the hippocampus (memory), but increased interaction with the dorsolateral cortex (thinking).

And so between emotional experience and memory storage, older participants inserted a thinking step. And with thought rather than emotion attached to bad memories, these memories were less immediately recalled.

GENIUS TESTER #12: DEMENTIA QUIZ

The following questions are from an e-mail widely circulated under the subject *dementia quiz*. And you thought you were smart . . .

QUESTION #1:

You're a participant in a race. You overtake the second person. What position are you in?

QUESTION #2:

You're a participant in a race. You overtake the last person. What position are you in?

QUESTION #3:

Do this in your head. No calculators! Take 1,000 and add 40 to it. Now add another 1,000. Now add 30. Add another 1,000. Now add 20. Now add another 1,000. Now add 10. What do you end up with?

QUESTION #4:

Mary's father has five daughters, four of whom are named Nana, Nene, Nini, and Nono. What is the name of the fifth daughter?

QUESTION #5:

A mute person goes into a shop and wants to buy a toothbrush. By imitating the action of brushing his teeth he successfully expresses himself to the shop-keeper and the purchase is made. Next, a blind man comes into the shop wanting to buy a pair of sunglasses; how does *he* indicate what he wants?

Zen Mind

Hogen asked four visiting monks, "There is a big stone. Do you consider it to be inside or outside your mind?"

One of the monks replied, "From the Buddhist viewpoint everything is an objectification of mind, so I would say that the stone is inside my mind."

"Your head must feel very heavy," observed Hogen.

THE FUNCTION OF DAYDREAMS

When we busy ourselves with mundane chores, our medial prefrontal cortex, posterior cingulated cortex, and the temporoparietal junction go to work. When we think through complex problems, it's the lateral prefrontal cortex and dorsal anterior cingulate cortex that light up on fMRI scans.

Only when we're daydreaming are *all* of the above areas active.

It's as if while daydreaming, we're able to integrate our creative with our workaday sides. You might not get the dishes done while staring blankly out the kitchen window, but you might suddenly find you understand relativity, or know exactly what's to be done in your love life.

MEAN STUFF IN THE NAME OF SCIENCE: LITTLE ALBERT

Pavlov discovered that dogs drool when they anticipate food.

If dogs could be taught to anticipate food at the sound of a bell, could they also be made to drool upon hearing the bell? Yes. This is classical conditioning.

Could the same be done with humans?

In 1920, psychologist John Watson and his assistant Rosalie Rayner of Johns Hopkins University hoped to find the answer. Their test subject was an eleven-month-old baby boy named Albert. Albert was allowed to play with a white pet rat, which at first he very much enjoyed. But then, whenever he actually touched the rat, Watson and Rayner began smacking a steel bar that was hung behind his crib, making a terrific noise and terrifying the hell out of poor little Albert. Eventually Albert learned to associate the rat with fear.

The good doctors insist they planned to desensitize Albert at the end of the study. But unfortunately, Albert left the study a month early. Nothing is known of Albert's later life.

This may be why psychology PhD students are now commonly required to have ethics committees evaluate dissertation proposals.

iDread

Peladophobia: fear of bald people.

The mind is like a parachute—it works only when it is open.

—Frank Zappa

I try to catch them right on the tip of his nose, because I try to punch the bone into the brain.

—Mike Tyson

iDread

Musophobia: fear of mice and rats.

Spiders are born knowing how to weave webs. It's little stretch to believe that humans, too, are born with instinct. And what is "instinct"? Is it cultural knowledge written in genetics? Accepting this definition of instinct is the first step down the long path of belief in humanity's shared experience—what some call the collective unconscious—and various people are willing to walk this path of belief for varying distances.

Let's take a mental stroll into the collective unconscious and test the stamina of your belief.

Carl Jung compared the mind to an onion (whereas Freud probably considered it a lotus blossom . . .). The heart of Jung's onion-mind is your individual brain, which is made up of your (thick) conscious and (thin) unconscious. The next layer is the mind you share with your family, with whom you're likely closest in belief, knowledge, and culture. Then the next layer of Jung's onion-mind is that of your culture, then your society, and finally a thin layer of mind shared with all of humanity.

He called this outermost layer the *collective unconscious*. Many of us live in only the onion's center. But that doesn't diminish the unconscious role of the onion's skin.

Again, if you're a massive curmudgeon, you can understand this through genetics: The architecture of your mind is similar to that of your family, and so you're likely to share ways of thought (and potentially, thoughts themselves).

Jung took this similarity of mind a rather large stride further. According to his theories, coded in his collective unconscious are not only physical instincts like the ability to weave a web, but the experiences basic to the human condition, too. To Jung, swirling around us are Beowulf and Shakespeare, Homer and *Star Wars*, the Vedas and the Bible—or more specifically, the *archetypes* that each of these taps into: We understand ourselves as balances of hero and servant, mother and victim, etc. How much scary-ass, half-robot father in a big black helmet do you have within yourself? How much Luke Skywalker?

And imbalance creates disorders: Too much "great mother" makes for a neurotic holiday season; too much "hero" makes it hard to stay retired from professional football.

Want proof? Jung (and Joseph

Disorders of the Collective Unconscious

Just as disorders can disrupt the individual mind, might they also be able to disrupt the collective mind? Extending the idea of mental disorder one "onion layer" outward, do certain families foster certain neuroticisms? Is a family OCD or ADHD or overly concerned with beauty and entitlement to the point of narcissism?

Could you extend the idea of disorder from individual, to family, to culture? Could a certain culture of North America be seen as just a wee bit narcissistic as a whole?

Eye Hack: Filling-in Illusion

Stare at the center dot. Let your mind go blank. Soon the outer circle should go blank too. This vanishing takes place to some degree whenever a visual stimulus is absolutely stable, and the filling-in always takes the color of the background.

Campbell) points to shared myths. Think of the Greek, Hindu, Native American, and Egyptian pantheons—certainly these cultures put their own spin on their gods, making them more or less aggressive, more or less sexual, and more or less idealized, but the archetypes these gods represent stay basically unchanged. They are part of our universal understanding.

Let's take another step down the C. U. path: You can access the collective unconscious. Yep, like Wi-Fi, our minds can tap into the information stream and pluck out URLs. Tapping into this archetypical understanding allows authors like Toni Morrison and Salman Rushdie to write stories that, while we don't quite know what the hell is going on, speak to "something deeper" within us.

And just as we pull archetypal understanding from the collective unconscious, Jung believes we can add to it: Do you believe that your actions contribute to a global consciousness? Does your holding the door open for the person behind you make the world a slightly better place? Do we add to or take from the great jar of karma?

But in addition to plucking the experience of archetype, this information drawn from the collective unconscious can also be just that: information (can't it?). Jung believed that each individual or culture uploads its information into the mainframe of the collective unconscious, and by tapping into this unconscious, we can know anything that has ever been known. Or we can learn of events or "feelings" far away in the world.

Some go even further. Take synchronicity. One day a client in Carl Jung's office was relating a dream of a scarab beetle and suddenly said beetle flew in the window. To Jung, these synchronous events were too perfect to be mere coincidence. Instead, the collective unconscious sent the beetle.

You still there? You want another step? Try this quote from the White Queen in *Through the Looking Glass:* "It's a poor sort of memory that only works backwards." If the collective unconscious knows humanity's shared past and present, why not its future, too?

OK, think about it: where did you get off the path of belief? Why did you jump? Are you *sure* you couldn't walk the path to its end?

ALGEBRAIC EIGHT-BALL: THE KARMOMETER— WOULD YOUR KARMA SURVIVE AN INTENDED PRANK?

- K = Your current karma estimate—on a scale of 1 to 10 with 1 being Pol Pot and 10 being Mother Teresa, how good of a person are you (excluding last year's April Fools' Day)?

- P = How deliciously good is the prank? (1 to 10 with 10 being "ultimate hilarity").

- G_N = The percentage of people who experienced or heard about the prank who, two days after the fact, did/would have a generally positive feeling about it.

- $V_\#$ = Number of victims.

- V_M = On average, how mad would each victim be just after the prank was pulled? (1 to 10 with 10 being "you'll need to have a witness protection program rep on speed dial").

- V_C = How close are you to the intended victim(s)? (1 to 10 with 10 being "my wife").

$$K - \left[\frac{2V_M(V_\# + V_C)}{P + \sqrt{G_N}} \right] = D_{oIt}$$

INTERPRETATION:

If D_{oIt} is less than -5, expect to be reincarnated as a nematode should you go through with your planned prank.

If D_{oIt} is between -5 and 0, you can hope for reincarnation as a lesser mammal.

If D_{oIt} is between 0 and 5, you should prank but then donate a kidney to restore karma.

If D_{oIt} is greater than 5, you can prank away without karmic repercussion.

BRAINWASHING THE EASY WAY

This is perhaps not the *nicest* entry in this book, and it definitely falls into the "you really shouldn't try this at home" category. That said, there's much to learn from Patty Hearst's kidnappers, cults, and the North Korean army. And with a little practice, you too can dehumanize friends and family to the point at which they're suscep-tible to your evil will. (Ominously, Philip Zimbardo writes, "Whatever any member of a cult has done, you and I could be recruited or seduced into doing.")

First the background:

Central to the definition of brainwashing is its ability to adjust not only our beliefs but also our values. It's not simply that we come to think that sacrificing the white-clad virgin Connie Swail will raise a god capable of destroying the world, but that we believe this is the right thing to do.

But the line between coercion into a cult and conversion into a religion is ambiguous. When is it brainwashing? Maybe it's at the point of consent—if you want to be washed then it's your right to be. But who's competent to make these decisions? Mental patients? Teenagers choosing to join a cult? Adults experiencing an evangelical "love bombing"?

And when does it stick? In the case of many Korean War prisoners, brainwashing proved to be more *playing along to avoid torture* than actual conversion to communist values. Interestingly, soldiers who originally had rigid belief systems were more likely to flip and adopt communism, while soldiers whose original beliefs were flexible were more likely to bend their beliefs while in captivity and spring back to their original values once released.

No matter the intention and results, the method remains largely the same:

The first and most important requirement is absolute control of the victim. No longer can the victim depend on him- or herself to fulfill basic needs; instead he or she needs you. Then dehumanize the victim, stripping away the self by systematically denying every descriptor—gender, profession, ethnicity, ideology, etc.—that the victim uses to define him- or herself. Eventually nothing of the victim's self remains but the intense notion that the self is bad. At this point, offer an alternative: communism, cultism, desperado-ism? Anything, really. And this system offers salvation: "Look, it's not you that's bad, it's your mistaken beliefs." And choosing the new beliefs allows the victim to rebuild a new, very different self.

Voilà: Automatons of the new world order? Aiders and abbeters of mayhem? Homicidal, blood-drinking hobos? With brainwashing, anything's possible.

Modern Dehumanization

Historically, equating races with animals has allowed slavery, internment, and extermination. But we've learned our lesson, right?

Implicit association tests—in which a subject responds to an image before executive function has the chance to override impulse—show that the answer is emphatically no. For example, one study found that participants paired faces of people living in traditional societies with animal- and childlike descriptive words. And in times of national stress, this dehumanization tends to bubble to the surface of the melting pot.

Test your own implicit associations and contribute to the research at implicit. harvard.edu/implicit/

Wild Kingdom: Amorous Ostriches

Does the captive ostrich experience Stockholm syndrome? Or is there another explanation for farm-raised ostriches' courtship behavior toward their human keepers? Is this phenomenon somehow funnier because the results were published in a journal called *British Poultry Science*?

FOUR STEPS TO PERSUASION

Want to make people do what you tell them? Here's how:

• Reason, but not too much reason: At a Kinko's, a customer asked to cut the long line for a copy machine, saying, "Can I jump the line because I need to make copies?" (Duh . . .) Another used the phrase "Can I jump the line, please?" The result? Ninety-three percent versus 24 percent success, respectively. But providing too many reasons or explanations decreases the power of any one reason. Researchers showed this by asking college students to come up with two or eight reasons why their test load shouldn't be increased. Those who came up with only two reasons were subsequently much more set against increased testing.

• Streamline: Cut *ummm, I mean, isn't it?*, and even the ubiquitous *like*. All equivocate and detract from the authority of your message. Also cut the overall time of your delivery. Researchers at the University of Sydney found that a long, hesitant pitch nixed sales for a scanner, even when the scanner was better and cheaper than others presented.

• Exploit weakness: Resistance requires effort. Hit your target when his defenses are down. Thus the late-night infomercial.

Or wait until he's hungry. If you need immediate results, blitz his mental resources before launching into your persuasion.

• Make it personal: Including a mint with the check increased tips 3.3 percent. When a waiter offered the mints himself, tips increased 14.1 percent. Likewise, researchers found that a handwritten Post-it note requesting a survey's return generated 39 percent more responses than a typed request. And face-to-face persuasion is much more effective than the same message via phone or e-mail.

LOGIC OF ILLOGIC: THE END IS NEAR

In the early 1950s, Chicago housewife Marian Keech trancewrote a message from aliens of the planet Clarion, warning that the world would end in a great flood just before dawn on December 21 of that year. On the fateful eve, believers gathered at Keech's house, having given away their possessions and removed all metal items from their persons (including bra straps) in preparation for flight aboard a midnight spacecraft that would land to save all true believers.

As you may have guessed by your continued existence, midnight came and went.

At 12:05 a.m., someone noticed that another clock said only 11:55. At 4:45 a.m., a despondent Keech trance-wrote another message, explaining that because of the small group's faith, God had spared the planet.

But illogically, the disproof of the group's doomsday prediction *strengthened* rather than *decreased* their belief.

What? Why? How?

Psychologists point to cognitive dissonance, the condition that results when our beliefs are contradicted by reality. When this happens, the brain must adjust in one of two ways: Either our beliefs need to change or reality needs to change, with the stronger of the two winning.

And so the members of Ms. Keech's cult, rather than changing their very strong beliefs, simply changed reality to fit them: Yes, aliens were all set to destroy the earth, but cultists' actions earned the benevolent intervention of God. Wow! In this framework, the eleventh-hour stay of earth execution proves the validity of their original beliefs—and their actions saved us all!

After that, who *wouldn't* jump on an apple crate at a busy Chicago street corner to spread the good word?

Zen Mind

Four pupils vowed to stay silent for seven days. When night came and the oil lamps were growing dim, one of the pupils could not help exclaiming to a servant, "Fix those lamps!"

The second pupil was surprised to hear the first one talk. "We are not supposed to say a word," he remarked.

"You two are stupid. Why did you talk?" asked the third.

"I am the only one who has not talked," concluded the fourth pupil.

WHIFFLE BALL CROTCH SHOT

We've all seen the home video show predicated on the idea that testicular damage is hilarious. But what's your first reaction when that affable dad takes a whiffle ball, toy airplane, golden retriever, piñata bat, donkey hoof, toddler's elbow, malfunctioning lawn chair, oar, rake, or Frisbee to the groin? First you wince. And it's quick: whack, wince, chuckle, repeat, for half an hour minus commercial breaks and a lead-in monologue for which even the host seems apologetic. We wince because of empathy: For a brief moment, we take the victim's pain as our own.

But what's our response to others' psychological or social pain? We don't wince immediately. Instead, our compassion takes longer to kick in. But once activated, it lingers longer than the vicarious pain of slapstick comedy.

SELF-TEST

Read the statements below and use a pencil to score each question's accuracy in describing your thoughts or behaviors, with one being "very inaccurate" and five being "very accurate." Flip to the back of the book for interpretation.

1. I am very aware of my surroundings.

2. I am able to fit in in any situation.

3. I have the ability to make others feel interesting.

4. I get puzzled by my own thoughts and feelings.

5. I know what makes others tick.

6. I get along well with people I have just met.

7. I don't know how to handle myself in a new social situation.

8. I am good at sensing what others are feeling.

9. I know what to say to make people feel good.

10. I am taken advantage of by others.

The picture's pretty bleak, gentlemen . . . The world's climates are changing, the mammals are taking over, and we all have a brain about the size of a walnut.

—Gary Larson, *The Far Side*

MUSIC, COMMERCE, AND MURDER

Psychologist Adrian North played either French or German classical music in the background of a wine shop. And depending on what music was playing, sales of French or German wine increased.

Similarly, researchers played classical or popular music in the background of a restaurant. And when classical music was playing, patrons spent 10 percent more, buying "sophisticated" entrées.

Also similarly, in the months of September, October, November, December, and sometimes January, PA systems in malls around the country play holiday music. And when shoppers hear the telltale *pa-rum-pum-pum-pum* we want to strangle the nearest elf. Maybe kick a reindeer.

But why, instead of feeling the holiday spirit coursing through us and reaching for our wallets, does the little drummer boy put us in mind of holiday homicide? In a (very funny) article in the *Wall Street Journal,* Daniel Levitin points to this music's acces-

sibility. A Bruckner symphony or the Beatles' *White Album* appeals to only the select few willing to put in the listening time needed to come to terms with the music's unexpected twists and turns. Holiday music, on the other hand, is meant to be immediately, universally appealing—we need to be charmed by the snippet we hear while walking past the window display at Macy's. But too much candy makes you sick. Without anything unexpected, our brains get bored. And the bored brain gets feisty. And homicidal. (This is also the reason we consider infanticide while riding It's a Small World.)

Interestingly, as culture evolves, the experimental can become the mainstream. When once Stevie Wonder was cutting edge, experimental, and aurally challenging, many of his tunes can now be heard on easy listening stations. His genius has been consumed and processed into palatability by the amoeba of pop culture. And post-Nirvana, classic hard rock can leave us feeling a bit blasé, but can you imagine listening to Jimi Hendrix with the ears of 1969?

iDread

Aulophobia: fear of flutes.

ALGEBRAIC EIGHT-BALL: WILL YOUR HOLIDAY CHEER SURVIVE HOLIDAY DINNER?

$$(R + S)\left(F + \frac{14P_T - P_T^2 + 1}{P_L + 1}\right)\left(\frac{D + 20}{T + D + 20}\right)^H = G_{obbleGobble}$$

P = How mad will your significant other be if you fight over turkey? (1 to 10 with 10 being "make you sleep on couch till next Turkey Day").

R = In dollars, how much is your least favorite guest likely to spend on your holiday present?

T = Hours you need to spend in close contact with this least favorite guest.

D = His or her general disapproval of your career and/or competence (0 to 10 with 0 being you're a "quarterback/surgeon/CEO/philanthropist" and 10 being you're a "ski-bum/pothead/hippie").

V = How vocal is he/she likely to be in this disapproval? (0 to 10 with 10 being "will refer to you only as *him, her,* or *so-and-so's husband,* as in 'can you please tell so-and-so's husband to pass me the yams?' ").

S = How sensitive are you (0–10 with 10 being "seismograph").

G$_{obbleGobble}$ is the percentage chance you *will* make it through holiday dinner without exploring alternate placements for the meat thermometer.

GAME THEORY MAKE BRAIN BIG: CAKE-CUTTING PROBLEM

You have four people and one cake. Obviously, the only fair way to divide the cake is to cut it into fourths. But what if a person is especially fond of frosting, or cherries, or marzipan? When is it worth trading quantity for quality?

What if instead of a cake, these people are France, Great Britain, the United States, and the USSR dividing Berlin after World War II? (Or Israel and Palestine dividing Jerusalem?)

As you might guess, real-world solutions can be massively complex. Since the beginning of recorded history, humans have used the strategy of one-divides, the-other-picks to divvy up finite resources. If you can think of a better way, the UN would love to hear it.

Will You Die This Year?

Statistical analysis of historical data shows a 100 percent chance that you will die. But what are your chances of dying this year? Scientists at Carnegie Mellon allow you to compute your chances and compare them with people in other demographics and areas. Visit deathriskrankings.com to see how seriously you should take this year's New Year's resolutions.

WILD KINGDOM: MOSQUITOES' DOUBLE DUTCH

Every year, malaria kills between one and three million people. Very rarely are any of these deaths in northern France, eastern Germany, or the Netherlands—the former territory of the Duchy of Limburg. This is somewhat surprising: The female malaria mosquito is highly attracted to the smell of Limburger cheese. In fact, mosquitoes' attraction to said cheese is equaled only by their attraction to the smell of human feet.

UN-APOLOGY APOLOGY

What to do when an apology's required but you feel less than apologetic? Or have been caught in the wrong and would rather bounce the blame than own it? Try the un-apology apology! The following strategies deflect the rays of wrongdoing like the S on Superman's chest. How many have you heard on CNN in the last week?

Wild Kingdom:
Impolite Herring

Do you remember the Jim Carrey movie in which he talks with his butt? Perhaps it's funny because it taps into humans' evolutionary memory of our past as sea dwellers —specifically, herring.

The simply truth is that herring cannot talk and so they fart. They do it at night, when they can't communicate by sight. And when a herring farts in the dark, other herring gather. A ball of farting herring can be millions strong. (Hippos communicate at night through defecation. . . .)

• Remove the specific act and yourself from it: "I think everyone knows that the misuse of taxpayer money is wrong. Anyone who does something like that is out of line."

• Question the harm done: "If my actions harmed anyone, I apologize."

• Truthfully confess to an unrelated charge: "I can honestly say that at no time during the unfortunate events with taxpayer money did I ever intend to use the money for my girlfriend's cosmetic procedures."

• Bury in technical jargon: "I regret my failure to conform to the specifications of the McCain-Feingold campaign finance reform act. There were instances in which I overlooked the subclauses governing the fair use of campaign contributions. I regret my lack of attention to the MFCFRA and assure voters that I will make every attempt to conform to the regulations in the future."

I regret deeply any injuries that may have been done in the course of the events that led to this decision. I would say only that if some of my judgments were wrong, and some were wrong, they were made in what I believed at the time to be the best interest of the nation.

—Richard Nixon,
resignation speech

• Passive voice makes the culprit disappear: "Unfortunately, it has been found that campaign contributions and taxpayer money were used in improper ways."

• Compare to a much worse possible outcome: "The thorough investigation found that, regardless of what you might have heard, no campaign contributors or taxpayers suffered any physical injury whatsoever."

• Oops, I made a mistake: "In hindsight, I realize that I made mistakes in the handling of campaign contributions. All of us make missteps and I want you to know how sorry I am for this lapse in judgment."

• Bonzai! Sometimes the best defense is a good offense: "Let me describe to you the recent, vicious attacks on me, my family, and on our great country, these United States of America, all by a sensationalist and biased media."

CHRISTMAS CAROLS FROM THE PSYCH COUCH

Schizophrenia—"Do You Hear What I Hear?"

Narcissism—"Hark! the Herald Angels Sing (About Me)"

Paranoia—"Santa Claus Is Coming to Get Me"

Obsessive-Compulsive Disorder—"Jingle Bell, Jingle Bell, Jingle Bell Rock. Jingle Bell, Jingle Bell, Jingle Bell Rock. Jingle Bell, Jingle Bell, Jingle Bell Rock. Jingle Bell, Jingle Bell, Jingle Bell Rock."

ANYTHING YOU CAN DO, I CAN DO BADDER

In economics, an exchange has an obvious value: You pay $2.59 and you get eggs. We call this the price. But in behavioral economics, it can be hard to price an exchange. What's the value of a good deed? What's the price of selfishness? If selfishness and generosity have equally large but opposite results, are they "priced" equally?

Psy-Op: Hands and Feet

Sit at the edge of a chair, lift your right foot, and spin your foot at the ankle in clockwise circles. Keep spinning. Now draw an imaginary "6" in the air with your right hand. Did your foot change directions?

Wait a minute: Economics? Behavior? Game theory? This sounds like a job for the University of Chicago! Indeed. In their quest to discover how we respond to generosity and selfishness and thus save us from the evil Lex Luthor, UC Supersleuths administered a series of giving and taking games on unsuspecting undergrads and the Chicagoan population at large.

In the first game, undergraduates played a giving game in which another player (actually a computer) generously gave each participant $50 of the computer's initial $100. In the next round, students started with $100 and decided how much to give the other player (the computer). On average they gave $49.50.

And so one good turn deserves another (minus only fifty cents).

Another group started with the $100 and the other player (computer) took away $50. Economically, this is exactly the same: In both cases the student was left with $50 after the first round. But in the following round, students took an average of $58 from the computer. Ha! That'll teach 'em to take away my money!

And so one perceived bad turn deserves another. And the response has eight bucks of added spite.

Great. But what happens in life, when we often get more than one turn each?

The intrepid UC Supersleuths recruited people from the mean streets of Chicago and assigned them seven rounds of either the giving or the taking game. This time people played face-to-face, mano a mano. In the first round, one player was secretly assigned to give or take $50, just as the computer had done. But in subsequent rounds, it was no holds barred for all.

What they found is cool: After multiple rounds of the giving game, players established trust and actually began giving more

Genius Tester #13: Gender Bias

In a certain country, boys are preferred. A couple will have children until they have a boy, at which point they stop having children. What is the proportion of boys to girls in this country?

than they kept, expecting the same in return the next round (implying there may be hope for the human race).

But as the game continued, players got increasingly greedy (and/or distrustful), working up to taking an average of $67 by the seventh round. Yikes.

In the next game, undergrads played one round of the giving or taking game, with one player assigned to be stingy (giving only $30 or taking $70), fair (giving or taking $50), or generous (giving $70 or taking $30). How would the other player respond? In fact, our aversion to having our stuff filched is so strong that the first player was seen as *more generous* when giving $30 than they were when taking $50.

But dammit Jim, what do all these games mean? For one, they demonstrate how failure to put the toilet seat down can quickly escalate to sleeping in the garage. Or how a cross-border skirmish can result in the whacking of the infamous red button. But it also implies that humanity must be fairly nice—if selfish actions have bigger consequences than fair or generous actions, in order to stay at equilibrium, we must be performing more generous than selfish actions.

The UC researchers also posit an evolutionary mechanism for

Zen Mind

A monk asked Zhaozhou to teach him.

Zhaozhou asked,
"Have you eaten your meal?"

The monk replied,
"Yes, I have."

"Then go wash your bowl," said Zhaozhou.

At that moment, the monk was enlightened.

"you scratch my back, and I'll scratch yours, but if you take my eye, I'll take both of yours," pointing out that this framework gently steers toward fairness and generosity (prosocial actions), while quickly and harshly correcting antisocial behavior.

Counter-productive Coercion

The goal of interrogation is to produce truthful memories. But researchers show that extreme stress (i.e., torture) has exactly the opposite effect: Repeated stress harms memory storage areas in the frontal lobe and encourages the formation of false memories. And stress releases hormones that bind to receptors in the hippocampus, blocking its ability to retrieve stored memories.

HOW TO *REALLY* SPOT A LIAR

You've seen the scene in a thousand noir movies: A lying suspect sweating, fidgeting, and slumping in a folding chair under a single, swinging bulb, while refusing to meet the eyes of the good or bad cop.

But research shows that liars do none of these things any more than do people telling the truth. Instead, the proof is in the pudding: It's a suspect's words themselves that tip the scale for fact or fiction.

And do you remember the cops that lay a verbal trap for a suspect, and when the suspect's tricked into contradicting himself, the investigators know they've got their man? Well, that's not how it works either. In fact, people telling the truth make *more mistakes* than people who are lying. Liars, as Benedict Carey writes in the *New York Times,* have learned to write a tight script and stick to it.

But the script's all they've got.

And so instead of the swinging lightbulb (and coercion with the goal of confession), the modern interrogation technique starts easy, with the suspect recollecting an unrelated, vivid memory, say, his or her wedding day. Only after hearing what a truthful memory sounds like do the investigators ask the suspect to recount the events in question. Then they have the suspect do it again, adding sounds, smells, and other sensory details. Then investigators make them recount the events in reverse.

Sequential Blind Lineup

You know the score: Six potential suspects stand against a wall and a witness tries to identify the real one. This process is prone to errors. Police accidentally (or intentionally) tip off the witness, and witnesses make relative judgments—they're going to pick somebody whether they're sure or not. Instead, police forces are now going double-blind sequential. This means that neither the officer nor the witness knows the real suspect. And "suspects" are presented one at a time. This forces witnesses to make absolute rather than relative judgments, evaluating their level of confidence in each person's guilt. An analysis of twenty-six studies found this method leads to 15 percent fewer identifications, but 39 percent fewer misidentifications.

Studies find that people telling the truth add 20 to 30 percent more extraneous details than liars. A truthful retelling puts the person in the moment of memory and with this moment come unrelated details that can't help but make their way into the story. A liar has no flood of memory. He or she has a narrow script.

If the story's too clean to be true, it's probably fake.

Office Decor: Beyond Feng Shui

Should you paint your office walls red or blue? If you're H&R Block, you should go red; if you're in the creative department of a marketing firm, go blue. That's because the color red increases performance on detail-oriented tasks, while blue enhances creativity.

RED BEATS BLUE AT THE OLYMPICS

In one-on-one Olympic competitions like boxing, tae kwon do, and wrestling, one competitor is assigned blue and the other is given red. They then box, kick, or grapple. With many events and many weight classes, you'd expect that blue would beat red as often as red beats blue. But that's not the case. In the 2004 Athens Olympics the competitor in red won in 57 percent of all tae kwon do matches. In boxing, red won 55 percent, and in wrestling, red won 53 percent of freestyle and 52 percent of Greco-Roman matches.

Think Alabama Crimson Tide, Manchester United, St. Louis Cardinals, Detroit Red Wings. Yes, think Michael Jordan.

All of these teams have a psychological edge over their opponents every time they step onto the field, court, or ice.

But why does red win?

One idea is the chicken-and-the-egg hypothesis that at one point a good team happened to wear red and other wannabe good teams copied their uniform.

But much more fun is to think that red actually weakens the opposition by signaling dominance (as it does in the animal world) or by disrupting rational thought (like a stop sign). Or maybe referees favor red.

To test this last theory, researchers at the University of Münster in Germany showed taped tae kwon do matches to a group of certified referees. Then they switched the color of the competitors' trunks and showed the exact tapes again. The verdict: The referees awarded the red-trunked competitor 13 per-cent more points than their blue-trunked rival, despite scoring exactly the same moves for each fighter.

Eye Hack:
Black and White in Color

The setup for this eye hack is a bit involved, but totally worth it. Copy and cut this pattern. Attach it to a CD or DVD. Spin the disc and look closely at the pattern. What do you see? (Or you can glue it to a spinning top.) Black and white should become color, though everyone sees different colors. If you can't see colors, you might have optic neuritis, an inflammation of the optic nerve.

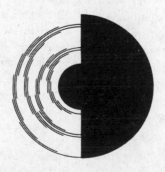

Have You Seen the Light?

Because the temporal lobe is the seat of emotion, seizure can also bring intense feelings of euphoria, fear, or ... rapture. A 2003 study published in the journal *Epilepsy & Behavior* describes the frequency of immediate religious conversion of people experiencing temporal lobe seizures.

What would the world be like today had Emperor Constantine—whose conversion and subsequent evangelism of the Roman empire followed a trembling vision of bright light—been quickly treated with a smelly shoe?

NEUROLOGICAL SUPPORT FOR THE USE OF SHOE SMELL IN CONTROLLING EPILEPTIC SEIZURE

For many hundreds of years, people in Eastern Europe have treated epileptic seizures with the quick administration of shoe smell. This smell (and specifically this smell) has the power to arrest the seizure, or so says the folk wisdom.

Fact or fiction?

If the brain were a boxing glove, the temporal lobe would be the thumb (your brain actually has two of these "thumbs," one on either side). The temporal lobe is the home of memory, speech, and hearing, and also houses the olfactory cortex, where we process smell. When the temporal lobe seizes, as it might during an epileptic incident, the onset is frequently marked by phantom smells, a condition called phantosmia (not to be confused with parosmia, in which a present smell is distorted).

Research published in the June 2008 issue of *Clinical Neurology and Neurosurgery* suggests that a strong smell administered just as a seizure starts functions like a slap to the face or the shock of defibrillation paddles to reset "truth" in the olfactory cortex, thereby stopping seizure in the temporal lobe. And in yesteryear's Eastern Europe, where the folk cure of shoe smell originated, shoes were made of tanned leather and likely to be crusted with mud, sweat, and a panoply of other various and sundry smells—in other words, shoes were the smelliest, most easily accessible things at hand in the cases of most epileptic seizures.

So there may be at least some truth to the folk cure.

Seizure and the Gender Switch

The journal *Epilepsy & Behavior* reports the case of a thirty-seven-year-old woman whose seizures give her the sense of becoming a man. During seizure, she believes she has a deeper voice and hairier arms. Researchers found damage in her right amygdala and surrounding right temporal lobe, which may be important pieces of the network that defines our sense of self and sexual identity.

PUZZLE ANSWERS

INTRO TO GAME THEORY: PRISONER'S DILEMMA

In this classic game-theory puzzle, the best thing you can do is to squeal like a pig. Imagine your sentences in the following possible scenarios:

• You remain silent, your partner squeals: ten years.

• You remain silent, your partner remains silent: six months.

• You squeal, your partner squeals: five years.

• You squeal, your partner stays silent: you walk.

So look, no matter if your partner squeals or if he stays quiet, your sentence is reduced if you squeal. Unfortunately, your partner's working with the same information. He's gonna squeal too, and you'll both end up with five years, when you both could have gotten six months if you'd both stayed quiet.

The prisoner's dilemma is an example of Nash equilibrium in which individuals act in their best interests and bring the situation to an equilibrium—but not necessarily the optimal one! If they'd cooperated instead of acting selfishly, they could have punched through Nash equilibrium into optimization.

The prisoner's dilemma has implications for social policy. Should every individual be left to fend for him- or herself (as in Ayn Rand's social Darwinism, where the fittest individuals prosper)? Or is the group bettered by mutual aid programs?

Should society be left to find its own Nash equilibrium, or should government provide incentives for desired behaviors?

GAME THEORY MAKE BRAIN BIG: COLONEL BLOTTO I

2,2,2 beats 1,1,4 and ties against all other strategies (1,2,3 and 2,2,2), so it "weakly dominates" all other choices and is Colonel Blotto's best strategy.

GAME THEORY MAKE BRAIN BIG: COLONEL BLOTTO II

2,4,6 ties 1,4,7 and 2,4,6 and 3,4,5 and 4,4,4, and beats the rest. Thus it "weakly dominates" all other choices and is Colonel Blotto's best strategy.

SELF-TEST: ROBIN HOOD MORALITY QUIZ

Find your answers in the following chart. RH = Robin Hood, LJ = Little John, MM = Maid Marian, SN = Sheriff of Nottingham. Percentages show people's common responses. Note: Figures are rounded to the nearest percentage.

RH, LJ, MM, SN	RH, LJ, SN, MM	RH, MM, LJ, SN	RH, MM, SN, LJ
A moralist with conventional ideas. Old-fashioned. 5% total.	Massively puritanical. Women conspire against men. 2% total.	Your philosophy is a confused mix of romanticism and moralism. 4% total.	You have high standards and are not predisposed to trust others. 2% total.

RH, SN, MM, LJ	RH, SN, LJ, MM	LJ, RH, MM, SN	LJ, RH, SN, MM
Ruthless authoritarian with weak personal morals. 2% total.	Misogynist! You see women as the possessions of men. 3% total.	Cautious and insecure—you distrust the opposite sex. 6% total.	Inferiority complex. Men: you fear women; women: get a backbone. 2% total.
LJ, MM, RH, SN	**LJ, MM, SN, RH**	**LJ, SN, MM, RH**	**LJ, SN, RH, MM**
You're a romantic, idealizing women or expecting too much of men. 15% total.	Slightly romantic realist. Broad-minded, flexible, and likely happy. 10% total.	You believe in common sense and relative morality. You're uncertain. 3% total.	Misogynist! You're a prude with an old-school opinion of women. 1% total.
MM, LJ, RH, SN	**MM, LJ, SN, RH**	**MM, RH, LJ, SN**	**MM, RH, SN, LJ**
Happy and well balanced. Some chivalry and/or high standards. 13% total.	Contented and maybe a little superior. Morality fits the occasion. 10% total.	You're guilty, lack confidence, and are overly concerned about others' opinions. 4% total.	Live a little! You're too stubborn. 1% total.
MM, SN, RH, LJ	**MM, SN, LJ, RH**	**SN, LJ, MM, RH**	**SN, LJ, RH, MM**
Women: you like your men strong and your women stronger. Men: wannabe lover. 2% total.	You're strong to the point of ruthlessness. Truth rules all. 3% total.	Sulky, confused, and immature. 2% total.	Men: you see women as fickle and inferior. Women: get a backbone. 1% total.
SN, MM, LJ, RH	**SN, MM, RH, LJ**	**SN, RH, MM, LJ**	**SN, RH, LJ, MM**
You claim to be a realist, but you're actually a romantic. 3% total.	A rebel with a trace of spoiled child. You value truth above morality. 2% total.	You prefer fantasy sex to real life. 3% total.	Men: You're afraid of women. Women: you like bad boys. 2% total.

SELF-TEST

This short test measures your trust. First add the scores for questions 1, 3, 4, and 7. Then subtract your scores for questions 2, 5, 6, and 8. The best way to interpret your score would be in comparison with those of other test-takers, but very generally, a positive score indicates that you're trustful while a negative score indicates you're distrustful.

GENIUS TESTER #1: WELL HUNG

At the end of each day, the prisoner can look forward and say *I must be executed on a later day,* allowing him to deduce the day of his execution and thus avoid execution ('cause he can't know the day ahead of time; if he does, he can't be executed). But this assumes he can make it to the end of the day. In other words, he can't ever rule out being executed in the present day. If days were inviolable chunks, he would survive, but they're not—he can be executed without warning at any time.

GENIUS TESTER #2: BRIDGE AND TORCH

It makes sense to put the torch in A's quick hands and let him/her run with it, shuttling people across and returning with the torch. But that takes 18 minutes: A takes B and then returns the torch: 3 minutes. A takes C and then returns alone: 6 minutes. A takes D: 9 minutes.

Better to stick the slowest people together, but with someone else to return the torch: A takes B and then returns the torch: 3 minutes. C and D cross together and then B returns the torch: 10 minutes. A and B sprint across together: 2 minutes, for a total of 15 minutes.

GENIUS TESTER #3: MEETING IN THE MIDDLE

Your best strategy is to leave very early and drive very fast—if you mashed the pedal at 5:30, you could perhaps make it home by 6:15. Even assuming you can't make the *whole* trip before your mom starts driving, you should still leave-early/drive-fast—the faster you drive, the less time it'll take to meet your mother on the way out, and your drive home will simply double this shortened time.

GENIUS TESTER #4: BOXES OF BARS

On the scale, place one bar from box number one, two bars from box two, three bars from box three, etc. Now the number of 20ths below the expected weight tells you which box is counterfeit.

GAME THEORY MAKE BRAIN BIG: KUHN POKER

If you bet, your opponent folds with a Jack or raises with a King. Half the time, you win your opponent's one-chip ante, and half the time you lose your ante plus your bet.

This is not good. In fact, it's bad. You're losing twice as many chips as you're winning.

So you check.

Now your opponent checks only if holding the Jack and you win. If your opponent bets he/she either has the King or is bluffing with the Jack. So calling this bet wins half the time (assuming your opponent is an ice-cold bluffer). If you call, you've got two chips versus two chips in a 50/50 pot; if you fold, you lose your ante every time.

So your best strategy when holding the Queen and playing first is to check and then call if necessary.

Serious game-theory geeks should search online for Steve Kuhn's description of three-card poker, in which he shows that with both players playing optimally, the first player loses 1/18th of his stack over time.

SELF-TEST: PERSONALITY SNAPSHOT

This self-test is one of the shortest scientifically accurate assessments of the "Big Five" personality factors: extraversion, agreeableness, conscientiousness, neuroticism, and intellect/imagination. While it's best to interpret these scores relative to other people taking the test, you can get an overview of your personality by looking for especially high and low scores, and noticing which of the five personality traits seem to outweigh others.

Here's how to score the test:

First, write your score (1 through 5) for each question next to that question's + or – mark.

Now you'll need to go through your answers one trait at a time; for instance, note that questions 1, 6, 11, and 16 are all marked "E." That means they all measure extraversion, and we'll need to combine our answers to them to get our extraversion score. Answers with a + mark in front of them should be added to your total score for a trait; those with a – mark should be subtracted. So, looking at extraversion again, you'd add your score for question 1, subtract your score for question 6, add your score for question 11, and subtract your score for question 16 to get your total extraversion score. Do the same with the remaining four traits. Which of the five do you score highest on? Lowest?

Number	Trait	Question	+ or −
1	E	Am the life of the party.	+ 3
2	A	Sympathize with others' feelings.	+ 5
3	C	Get chores done right away.	+ 4
4	N	Have frequent mood swings.	+ 1
5	I	Have a vivid imagination.	+ 4
6	E	Don't talk a lot.	− 2

Number	Trait	Question	+ or −
7	A	Am not interested in other people's problems.	− 2
8	C	Often forget to put things back in their proper place.	− 2
9	N	Am relaxed most of the time.	− 2
10	I	Am not interested in abstract ideas.	− 1
11	E	Talk to a lot of different people at parties.	+ 4
12	A	Feel others' emotions.	+ 4
Number	Trait	Question	+ or −
13	C	Like order.	+ 4
14	N	Get upset easily.	+ 1
15	I	Understand abstract ideas.	+ 4
16	E	Keep in the background.	− 2
17	A	Am not really interested in others.	− 2
18	C	Make a mess of things.	− 1
19	N	Seldom feel blue.	− 2
20	I	Do not have a good imagination.	− 1
Total E—Extraversion			3
Total A—Agreeableness			5
Total C—Conscientiousness			4
Total N—Neuroticism			−2
Total I—Intellect/Imagination			6

16

GENIUS TESTER #5: MR. SMITH'S CHILDREN

Did you say 50/50 both times? Wrong! Imagine the four possibilities for a two-child family: girl-girl, girl-boy, boy-girl, and boy-boy. In the first case, we know the first child's a girl, so we can cross off the last two options (boy-girl and boy-boy), leaving the options girl-girl and girl-boy. OK, in this case you're right: there *is* a 50 percent chance the second child's a girl.

Now let's look at the second case.

If we know that "at least one of them is a boy," we can cross off only girl-girl, leaving girl-boy, boy-boy, and boy-girl. Notice that only one of the remaining three scenarios is boy-boy. As counterintuitive as it may seem, after specifying that "one child is a boy," there's only a one-in-three or 33 percent chance that both are.

GAME THEORY MAKE BRAIN BIG: GUESS TWO-THIRDS OF THE AVERAGE

Well, the maximum possible average of numbers from 0 to 100 is 100 and so you're certainly not going to guess above 66.67 (which is ⅔ of 100). You can be assured that the other game theory experts in your guessing group aren't going to guess above 66.67 either. So you can consider 66.67 the maximum possible guess. Now the maximum you'd want to guess is two-thirds of *that,* or 44.45. And that's true for everyone. So now you can be assured that no one will guess over 44.45. Eventually, you can extend this reasoning all the way to 0, which is your best guess.

In practice, the winning guess in a Dutch version of this game, which drew almost 20,000 entries, was 21.6. Apparently, not every Netherlander is versed in game theory.

GENIUS TESTER #6: FOUR SQUARES PROBLEM

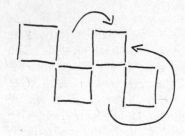

SELF-TEST

This short test measures your happiness. First add the scores for questions 2, 3, 6, 8, and 10. Then subtract your scores for questions 1, 4, 5, 7, and 9. The best way to interpret your score would be in comparison with those of other test-takers, but very generally, a positive score indicates that you're more happy than sad.

GENIUS TESTER #7: MISSING BOX

Look at the puzzle pieces. Included are two right triangles,

one 5 x 2 and another 8 x 3. Here's the thing: Their hypotenuses (top sides, here) sit at slightly different angles. And so when we stack these triangles tip-to-top as in this puzzle, it creates a very slight bend in the hypotenuse of the resulting, larger "triangle." We're used to seeing right triangles, so we don't notice it. So the hypotenuse of the top figure caves slightly inward, while the hypotenuse of the lower figure bends slightly up, allowing the bottom figure a little more area than the top. Thus the extra box.

GAME THEORY MAKE BRAIN BIG: EL FAROL BAR

The catch-22 is that any "best" strategy is doomed to fail: If everyone decides to stay home, the bar will be empty and thus fun; if everyone decides to go, the bar will be crowded and people should've stayed home.

And so the best strategy is a mixed strategy in which each person has a set probability of going. The probability depends on how many people are deciding, the capacity of the bar, and how close the experience of staying home is to the experience of going to the bar.

If you can communicate and lie, you should say that you're going to the bar, every time. If you end up going, your truth may have scared others away; if you stay home, your lie hasn't hurt you at all.

EYE HACK: SATIRE ON FALSE PERSPECTIVES

- The man in the foreground's fishing rod's line passes behind that of the man behind him.

- The sign is moored to two buildings, one in front of the other, with beams that show no difference in depth

- The sign is overlapped by two distant trees.

- The man climbing the hill is lighting his pipe with the candle of the woman leaning out of the upper story window.

- The crow perched on the tree is massive in comparison with it.

GAME THEORY MAKE BRAIN BIG: PIRATE PUZZLE

Believe it or not, the pirate king need only split the 100 gold pieces as follows: 98 for himself, none for B, one for C, none for D, and one for E.

Imagine it came down to pirates D and E. D could keep all the gold, with the one-to-one tied vote falling in his favor. E knows this.

And so does C. So C only needs to offer E one gold piece to ensure E's vote (that's one more than E would get otherwise).

But B knows this too. So B offers D one gold to ensure D's vote and the tie.

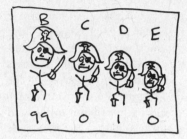

But pirate king A hasn't become pirate king for nothing. He's a craftily rational pirate and has the game aced: He ensures a 3/2 split in his favor by offering a gold piece each to C and E, which is exactly one more than they would get for throwing the king overboard.

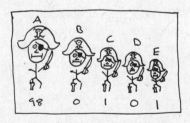

HANDWRITING ANALYSIS

1. Mahatma Gandhi. 2. Walt Whitman. 3. Fidel Castro. 4. Abraham Lincoln. 5. Jane Austen. 6. The Zodiac killer. 7. Jack the Ripper. 8. Charles Darwin.

GENIUS TESTER #8: HOUSES & UTILITIES

In two dimensions, it's impossible. Exactly one line has to cross one other. But imagine the houses and utilities placed on a 3-D shape like a donut. This allows you to connect the one tricky line, house to utility, by wrapping around the donut's outer edge and reentering through the center (electricity to house #3 in this picture).

GAME THEORY MAKE BRAIN BIG: NASH BARGAINING GAME

Ha! There is no solution! Did that hurt your brain? With prior knowledge of your opponent, you might be able to guess if he or she is likely to demand more or less than half the pot. But that's the best you can do: guess.

SELF-TEST

This short test measures your conservatism. First add your scores for questions 1, 2, 4, 6, and 7. Then subtract your scores for questions 3, 5, and 8. The best way to interpret your scores would be in relation to those of other test-takers, but very generally, a score above 6 implies you are more conservative than not.

SELF-TEST

This short test measures your honesty. First add your scores for questions 2, 3, 6, and 8. Then subtract your scores for questions 4, 7, 10, and 11 (numbers 1, 5, and 9 are not scored). The best way to interpret your scores would be in relation to those of other test-takers, but very generally, a positive score implies honesty.

PSY-OP: PICK A NUMBER, ANY NUMBER

The number you picked is 7. Pretty cool, eh? Addition wipes your mind free of distraction, priming you to subtract 5 from 12.

GENIUS TESTER #9: THE PSYCHOLOGY OF GETTING SUCKERED

No matter what cards he has, Jonathan will always be able to turn over two non-ace cards.

Showing those two cards has no effect on the probability that one of his three cards is an ace. But most people can't help but treat the remaining cards as equally likely to be an ace, and therefore they (incorrectly) calculate the chances of Jonathan's hand containing an ace as one-third. So, very few wanted to switch hands with him.

The correct answer, of course, is to switch hands, earning the original three-to-five odds.

GAME THEORY MAKE BRAIN BIG: DINER'S DILEMMA

In game theory, a pure strategy is one in which you act in a certain way every time. There are two pure strategies in the Diner's Dilema: expensive meal every time or cheap meal every time. Playing the pure strategy of the expensive meal means that after everyone eats phat, splitting the bill results in everyone paying exactly the price of the expensive meal (which we already said wasn't worth it). But playing the other pure strategy (everyone orders cheap), you never "win" any utility over the baseline. Techni-

cally, these two pure strategies are equal: In both, you get what you pay for.

And so a mixed strategy might be best, with some people ordering cheap and others ordering expensive. The exact mix depends on how much individuals value the expensive meal (compared with its price), how many people are in the group, etc.

PSY-OP: VEGGIE MATH

Did you think of a carrot? Yes, a carrot looks much like a downward-pointing arrow.

GAME THEORY MAKE BRAIN BIG: PEACE/ WAR

If you were playing mano a mano, the best strategy would be the pure one of war all the time. You would either tie (1,1) or win outright (3,0). You would forgo earning a long string of two-point peace/peace ties, but you would beat or tie your opponent. This is what Genghis Khan did. It's what the Vikings did, too: you know, all that burning and pillaging.

But constant war works only until the surrounding countries get hip. And when they do, they team up to punish the aggressor. In the Vikings' case, this team was called the Hanseatic League, which played a strategy that game theorists call the "provocable nice guy." This strategy shoots "peace" the first round and then mimics the opponent's actions every round thereafter. The majority of peaceful nations gain wealth through cooperation, while every round, the aggressor is attacked by the nation it attacked last time (a bit like many swallows worrying a hawk).

A refinement of the provocable nice guy is "provocable nice guy with a touch of forgiveness." This adds an infrequent "peace" in the round after an opponent shoots "war," and can break an escalating cycle of aggression.

GENIUS TESTER #10: TIME TRAVEL

1. The clock hands show it five minutes ahead.

2. If the entire clock is stopped in time, then it no longer exists in the present. Poof, it's gone!

3. The hands remain unchanged but its existence skips ahead: you have to wait five minutes to see it.

GENIUS TESTER #11: THE MONTY HALL PROBLEM

This is just a bit tricky, so dig in:

Most people think that you originally have a one-third chance and that after seeing a goat in an open door, you have a half a chance and so you might as well stick with your original choice.

Most people are wrong. Imagine the three possible choices and the results of switching (see page 230):

Choice	Switch	Result
1.		**Bad!** If the participant picks the car, sees a goat, and switches, he loses.
2.		**Good!** If the participant picks a goat and sees a goat, switching wins the car.
3.		**Good!** If the participant picks a goat and sees a goat, switching wins the car.

So switching results in a win two out of three times. A study of 228 people found that only 13 percent switched and that the vast majority of these did so thinking they still had a 50/50 chance.

GENIUS TESTER #12: DEMENTIA QUIZ

Question #1: Second.
Question #2: Um, how can you overtake the *last* person?
Question #3: 4,100. (What, did you get 5,000? Check your math.)
Question #4: Mary. Duh.
Question #5: He opens his mouth and asks for it.

SELF-TEST

This short test measures your emotional intelligence. First add your scores for questions 2, 3, 5, 6, 8, and 9. Then subtract your scores for question 7 (questions 1, 4, and 10 are not scored). The best way to interpret your score would be in comparison with those of other test-takers, but very generally, a score above 15 implies you are fairly emotionally intelligent.

GENIUS TESTER #13: GENDER BIAS

Because every couple eventually has exactly one boy, if there are x number of couples, there will be x boys. Done.

Now imagine the number of girls:

Half the couples have a girl first, so $x/2$ girls are born in this first "generation." The chance of having two girls in a row is one in four, so of the couples who have to try again, $x/4$ girls are born. The chance of having three girls in a row is one in eight, so $x/8$ girls are born. So the total number of girls is $x/2 + x/4 + x/8 + x/16$, etc. Eventually this all adds up to one.

So the ratio of boys-to-girls in this country is one-to-one.

REFERENCES

COUNTRY MUSIC KILLS

Stack, Steven, and Jim Gundlach. "The Effect of Country Music on Suicide." *Social Forces* 71, no. 1 (September 1992):211–218.

BE NICE, BUT NOT TOO NICE: GAME THEORY SAYS SO

Axelrod, Robert, and William D. Hamilton. "The Evolution of Cooperation." *Science* 211, no. 4489 (March 27, 1981):1390–96.

SOCIAL CONTAGION: HAPPINESS AND OBESITY ARE CATCHING

Thompson, Clive. "Is Happiness Catching?" *New York Times Magazine* (September 13, 2009):28.

BOOZE PROTECTS THE BRAIN

Anstey, Kaarin J., Holly Mack, and Nicolas Cherbuin. "Alcohol Consumption as a Risk Factor for Dementia and Cognitive Decline: Meta-Analysis of Prospective Studies." *American Journal of Geriatric Psychiatry* 17, no. 7 (July 2009):542–555.

TOO DUMB TO KNOW IT

Kruger, Justin, and David Dunning. "Unskilled and Unaware of It: How Difficulties in Recognizing One's Own Incompetence Lead to Inflated Self-Assessments." *Journal of Personality and Social Psychology* 77, no. 6 (1999):1121–1134.

SMARTER EVERY DAY

Flynn, James R. *What Is Intelligence?: Beyond the Flynn Effect*. New York: Cambridge University Press, 2009. Expanded edition.

Carr, Nicholas. "Is Google Making Us Stupid?" *Atlantic Monthly* 302, no. 1 (July 2008):56–63.

THE KEY TO BRAIN TRAINING

Woolston, Chris. "Do Brain Workouts Sharpen Thinking?" *Los Angeles Times* (August 24, 2009). latimes.com/features/health/la-he-brain-fitness24-2009aug24,0,6799758.story.

THE GUILTY PLEASURE OF SCHADENFREUDE

Takahashi, Hidehiko et al. "When Your Gain Is My Pain and Your Pain Is My Gain: Neural Correlates of Envy and Schadenfreude." *Science* 323, no. 5916 (February 13, 2009):937–939.

MIRROR NEURONS: YOUR ACTIONS IN MY HEAD

Iacoboni, Marco. *Mirroring People: The New Science of How We Connect with Others*. New York: Farrar, Straus & Giroux, 2008.

WILD KINGDOM: SENTIENT ELEPHANTS

Plotnik, Joshua M., Frans B. M. de Waal, and Diana Reiss. "Self-recognition in an Asian Elephant." *Proceedings of the National Academy of Sciences of the United States of America* 103, no. 45 (November 07, 2006):17053–17057.

NEURAL NETS KNOW ALL

Chen, Yuehui, Bo Yang, and Ajith Abraham. "Flexible Neural Trees Ensemble for Stock Index Modeling." *Neurocomputing* 70, no. 4–6 (January 2007):697–703.

Zaknich, Anthony, and Sue K. Baker. "A Real-Time System for the Characterisation of Sheep Feeding Phases from Acoustic Signals of Jaw Sounds." *Australian Journal of Intelligent Information Processing Systems (AJIIPS)* 5, no. 2, (Winter 1998): 000–000.

BRAIN CHIP: NEURAL NETS AND THE ARTIFICIAL HIPPOCAMPUS

Berger, T. W. et al. "Restoring Lost Cognitive Function." *Engineering in Biology and Medicine* 24, no. 5 (Sept.–Oct., 2005):30–44.

Graham-Rowe, Duncan. "The World's First Brain Prosthesis Revealed." *New Scientist* 177, no. 2386 (March 15, 2003):4.

PIECE OF MIND: HIPPOCAMPUS

Dalla, Christina, et al. "Neurogenesis and Learning: Acquisition and Asymptotic Performance Predict How Many New Cells Survive in the Hippocampus." *Neurobiology of Learning and Memory* 88, no. 1 (July 2007):143–148.

ABNORMAL PSYCH: HM (PATIENT)

Corkin, Suzanne. "What's New with the Amnesic Patient H.M.?" *Nature Reviews Neuroscience* 3, no. 2 (February 2002):153–160.

Carey, Benedict. "H. M., an Unforgettable Amnesiac, Dies at 82." *New York Times* (December 4, 2008), 1.

SPEED SHRINKING

"Speed Shrinking." *Publishers Weekly* 256, no. 22 (June 2009):33.

LOGIC OF ILLOGIC: THE TRICKY SECONDARY MARKET AND WHY ECONOMISTS HATE PSYCHOLOGY

Carmon, Ziv, and Don Ariely. "Focusing on the Forgone: How Value Can Appear So Different to Buyers and Sellers." *Journal of Consumer Research* 27 (December 2000):360–370.

Seabrook, John. "The Price òf the Ticket." *New Yorker* (August 10, 2009):34.

COGNITIVE COSTS OF WINNING AND LOSING ROCK, PAPER, SCISSORS

Kikuchi, Senichiro, et al. "Prefrontal Cerebral Activity During a Simple 'Rock, Paper, Scissors' Task Measured by the Noninvasive Near-Infrared Spectroscopy Method." *Psychiatry Research: Neuroimaging* 156, no. 3 (December 15, 2007):199–208.

Goudriaan, Anna E., et al. "Neurocognitive Functions in Pathological Gambling: A Comparison with Alcohol Dependence, Tourette Syndrome and Normal Controls." *Addiction* 101, no. 4 (April 2006):534–547.

THE HEDONOMETER

Dodds, Peter, and Christopher Danforth. "Measuring the Happiness of Large-Scale Written Expression: Songs, Blogs, and Presidents." *Journal of Happiness Studies* (July 17, 2009):1389.

LOGIC OF ILLOGIC: BRAIN-DEFLATING FALLACIES TO WIN ANY ARGUMENT, PARTS I–IV

Pope, Kenneth. "Logical Fallacies in Psychology: 21 Types." (2003): kspope.com/fallacies/fallacies.php.

THE CALCULUS OF COMPASSION

Darley, John M., and Bibb Latané. "Bystander Intervention in Emergencies: Diffusion of Responsibility." *Journal of Personality and Social Psychology* 8 (April 1968):377–383.

Piliavin, J. A., J. F. Dovidio, S. L. Gaertner, and R. D. Clark. *Emergency Intervention.* New York: Academic Press, 1981.

GAME THEORY MAKE BRAIN BIG: THE ORIGIN OF FAIRNESS

Forsythe, R., J. Horowitz, N. E. Savin, and M. Sefton. "Fairness in Simple Bargaining Experiments." *Games and Economic Behavior* 6 (May 1994):347–369.

Güth, Werner, Rolf Schmittberger, and Bernd Schwarze. "An Experimental Analysis of Ultimatum Bargaining." *Journal of Economic Behavior & Organization* 3, no. 4 (December 1982):367–388.

THE SMELL OF TRUST

Kosfeld, Michael, et al. "Oxytocin Increases Trust in Humans." *Nature* 435 (June 2, 2005):673–676.

WILD KINGDOM: MARTYRDOM IN BREWER'S YEAST

Keller, Laurent, and Kenneth G. Ross. "Selfish Genes: A Green Beard in the Red Fire Ant." *Nature* 394 (August 6, 1998):573–575.

BUT WHAT DO THE VOICES SAY?

Hayward, Mark. "Daring to Talk Back." *Mental Health Practice* 10, no. 9 (June 2007):12–15.

HEAR WITH YOUR EYES, SPEAK WITH YOUR EARS

Ito, Takayuki, Mark Tiede, and David J. Ostry. "Somatosensory Function in Speech Perception." *Proceedings of the National Academy of Sciences of the United States of America* 106, no. 4 (January 27, 2009):1245–1248.

Probst, R., et al. "Spontaneous, Click-, and Toneburst-Evoked Otoacoustic Emissions from Normal Ears." *Hearing Research* 21, no. 3 (1986):261–75.

PIECE OF MIND: TEMPORAL LOBE

Chan, Dennis, et al. "The Clinical Profile of Right Temporal Lobe Atrophy." *Brain: A Journal of Neurology* 132, no. 5 (May 2009):1287–1298.

PSY-OP: FLEXIBLE MIND OF MASTERY

Bilalić, Merim, Peter McLeod, and Fernand Gobet. "Inflexibility of Experts— Reality or Myth? Quantifying the Einstellung Effect in Chess Masters." *Cognitive Psychology* 56, no. 2 (March 2008):73–102.

PERSIAN COW PRINCE

Haque, Amber. "Psychology from Islamic Perspective: Contributions of Early Muslim Scholars and Challenges to Contemporary Muslim Psychologists." *Journal of Religion and Health* 43, no. 4 (December 2004):357–377.

THE EXPRESSIVE BODY

Buscombe, Richard, et al. "Expectancy Effects in Tennis: The Impact of Opponents' Pre-Match Non-Verbal Behaviour on Male Tennis Players." *Journal of Sports Sciences* 24, no. 12 (December 2006):1265–1272.

Schindler, Konrad, Luc Van Gool, and Beatrice de Gelder. "Recognizing Emotions Expressed by Body Pose: A Biologically Inspired Neural Model." *Neural Networks* 21, no. 9 (November 2008): 1238–1246.

Willems, Roel M., and Peter Hagoort. "Neural Evidence for the Interplay Between Language, Gesture, and Action: A Review." *Brain and Language* 101, no. 3 (June 2007):278–289.

SHORT AND STOUT, LONG AND TALL

Wansink, Brian, and Koert van Ittersum. "Bottoms Up! The Influence of Elongation and Pouring on Consumption Volume." *Journal of Consumer Research* 30, no. 3 (December 2003):455–463.

PIECE OF MIND: HYPOTHALAMUS

Bruce, Hilda. "An Exteroceptive Block to Pregnancy in the Mouse." *Nature* 184, no. 105 (July 11, 1959).

LOGIC OF ILLOGIC: ANCHORING

Rosenwald, Michael S. "Putting Prices Into Focus." *Washington Post*, June 22, 2008:F01.

Teach, Edward. "Avoiding Decision Traps: Cognitive Biases and Mental Shortcuts Can Lead Managers into Costly Errors of Judgment." *CFO* magazine (June 1, 2004).

OUIJA TWEET BRAIN INTERFACE

"Your Brain On Twitter: No Hands Necessary." April 4, 2009. npr.org/templates/story/story.php?storyId=103457130&ft=1&f=1001

DEBUNKED: SELF-AFFIRMATION STINKS

Wood, Joanne V., W. Q. Elaine Perunovic, and John W. Lee. "Positive Self-Statements: Power for Some, Peril for Others." *Psychological Science* 20, no. 7 (July 2009):860–866.

THE ECONOMICS OF MATING I–IV

Barber, Nigel. "Women's Dress Fashions as a Function of Reproductive Strategy." *Sex Roles* 40, no. 5–6 (April 1999):459–471.

Kruger, Daniel J., and Eric Schlemmer. "When Men Are Scarce, Good Men Are Even Harder to Find: Life History, the Sex Ratio, and the Proportion of Men Married." *Journal of Social, Evolutionary, and Cultural Psychology* 3, no. 2 (2009): 93–104.

Marlowe, F. "Paternal Investment and the Human Mating System." *Behavioural Processes* 51, no. 1–3 (October 5, 2000):45–61.

BOYS HAVE COOTIES

Thomas, Abbie, and Georgina Hickey. "The Big Die Young." *Nature Australia* 27, no. 10 (Spring 2003): 14.

PARASITE BRAIN PUNK

Dogruman-Al, Funda, et al. "A Possible Relationship Between *Toxoplasma gondii* and Schizophrenia: A Seroprevalence Study." *International Journal of Psychiatry in Clinical Practice* 13, no. 1 (March 2009):82–87.

"Parasites: The Scratch." *Radiolab.* WNYC New York Public Radio. New York, NY: September 25, 2009. wnyc.org/shows/radiolab/episodes/2009/09/25/segments/133981.

Yereli, Kor, I. Cüneyt Balcioğlu, and Ahmet Özbilgin. "Is *Toxoplasma gondii* a Potential Risk for Traffic Accidents in Turkey?" *Forensic Science International* 163, no. 1–2 (November 10, 2006):34–37.

HANG UP AND DRIVE: YOUR BRAIN, SPLIT

Just, Marcel Adam, Timothy A. Keller, and Jacquelyn Cynkar. "A Decrease in Brain Activation Associated with Driving When Listening to Someone Speak." *Brain Research* 1205 (April 18, 2008):70–80.

WZ Arrive. "Multitasking—Bad for the Brain?" *Science* 325, no. 5944 (August 28, 2009):1053.

Salvucci, Dario D., and Kristen L. Macuga. "Predicting the Effects of Cellular-Phone Dialing on Driver Performance." *Cognitive Systems Research* 3, no. 1 (March 2002):95–102.

WILD KINGDOM: HUMMINGBIRDS VS. FIGHTER PILOTS

Milius, Susan. "Hummingbird Pulls Top Gun Stunts." *Science News* 176, no. 1 (July 4, 2009):7.

PIECE OF MIND: FRONTAL LOBE

Gomez-Beldarrain, Marian, et al. "Patients with Right Frontal Lesions Are Unable to Assess and Use Advice to Make Predictive Judgments." *Journal of Cognitive Neuroscience* 16, no. 1 (January 2004):74–89.

WILD KINGDOM: THE RED-NECKED PHALAROPE

Schamel, Douglas, Diane M. Tracy, and David B. Lank. "Male Mate Choice, Male Availability and Egg Production as Limitations on Polyandry in the Red-Necked Phalarope." *Animal Behaviour* 67, no. 5 (May 2004):847–853.

LOGIC OF ILLOGIC: BATTLE ROBOT

Aronson, Elliot, and J. Merrill Carlsmith. "Effects of the Severity of Threat on the Devaluation of Forbidden Behavior." *Journal of Abnormal and Social Psychology* 66 (June 1963):584–588.

WILD KINGDOM: RECREATIONAL RAT PHARMACOPEIA

Chiara, G.D., and A. Imperato. "Drugs Abused by Humans Preferentially Increase Synaptic Dopamine Concentrations in the Mesolimbic System of Freely Moving Rats." *Proceedings of the National Academy of Sciences* 85, no. 14 (July 1, 1988):5274–5278.

EYE HACK: THE WATERFALL ILLUSION

Konkle, Talia, et al. "Motion Aftereffects Transfer between Touch and Vision." *Current Biology* 19, no. 9 (May 12, 2009):745–750.

CLOWNS' SELF-PURPOSE

Fisher, Seymour, and Rhoda Fisher. *The Psychology of Adaptation to Absurdity: Tactics of Make-Believe.* Hillsdale, NJ: Lawrence Erlbaum Associates, 1993.

NAILS AND THE HUMAN BRAIN

"Cause of Man's Toothache? A 4-Inch Nail." *New York Times* (January 17, 2005): 13.

Schwarzschild, Michael. "Nail in the Brain." *New England Journal of Medicine* 328, no. 9 (March 4, 1993):620.

"Oregon Man Survives 12 Nails to the Head." Associated Press. Portland, Ore. (April 21, 2006). msnbc.msn.com/id/12425803/

Demetriades, A. K., and M. C. Papadopoulos. "Penetrating Head Injury in Planned and Repetitive Deliberate Self-Harm." *Mayo Clinic Proceedings* 82 (May 2007):536.

"Doctor Uses Claw Hammer to Remove 2.5-Inch Nail From Man's Head." Fox News. Shawnee, Kan. (June 11, 2008): foxnews.com/story/0,2933,365655,00.html.

NOT BY NAILS ALONE

Mandat, T. S., C. R. Honey, D. A. Peters, and B. K. Sharma. "Artistic Assault: An Unusual Penetrating Head Injury Reported as a Trivial Facial Trauma." *Acta Neurochirurgica* 147, no. 3 (March 2005): 331–333.

Karabatsou, K., J. Kandasamy, and N. G. Rainov. "Self-Inflicted Penetrating Head Injury in a Patient with Manic-Depressive Disorder." *American Journal of Forensic Medicine and Pathology* 26 (2005):174–6.

JOCKS, NERDS, AND THE SECRETS OF SUCCESS

Simonton, Dean Keith, and Anna V. Song. "Eminence, IQ, Physical and Mental Health, and Achievement Domain: Cox's 282 Geniuses Revisited." *Psychological Science* 20, no. 4 (April 2009):429–434.

BUT JOCKS GET BETTER GRADES

French, Michael, et al. "Effects of Physical Attractiveness, Personality, and Grooming on Academic Performance in High School." *Labour Economics* 16 (August 2009):373–382.

Sparacino, Jack, and Stephen Hansell. "Physical Attractiveness and Academic Performance: Beauty Is Not Always Talent." *Journal of Personality* 47, no. 3 (September 1979):449–469.

ATKINS MAKES YOU DUMB?

D'Anci, Kristen E., et al. "Low-Carbohydrate Weight-Loss Diets. Effects on Cognition and Mood." *Appetite* 52, no. 1 (February 2009):96–103.

CORTICAL HOMUNCULUS

Ramachandran, V. S. *A Brief Tour of Human Consciousness*. New York: Pi Press, 2004.

RISK AVERSION IN ACTION

Post, Thierry, Martijn J. van den Assem, Guido Baltussen, and Richard H. Thaler. "Deal or No Deal? *Decision-making under Risk in Large-Payoff Game Show.*" *American Economic Review* 98, no. 1 (March 2008):38–71.

LOGIC OF ILLOGIC: LUXURY BLOODLUST

Trei, Lisa. "Price Tag Can Change the Way People Experience Wine, Study Shows." Stanford News Service: news-service.stanford.edu/pr/2008/pr-wine-011608.html.

GAME THEORY MAKES MY BRAIN HURT: KUHN POKER

Kuhn, H. W. "Simplified Two-Person Poker." In *Contributions to the Theory of Games,* volume 1. Pages 97–103. Princeton, NJ: Princeton University Press, 1950.

AUTHORITY AND THE STRIP SEARCH PRANK CALL

Gease, Heidi Bell. "Fla. Man Arrested in Strip Search Hoax Calls." *Rapid City Journal,* online edition (July 7, 2004): www.rapidcityjournal.com/news/local/article_59123bfc-3ff3-5995-8af7-866fb9d15b0.html.

AH, THE TEENAGE (Y)EARS

Vitello, Paul, with contribution from Kate Hammer and Nate Schweber. "A Ring Tone Meant to Fall on Deaf Ears." *New York Times* (June 12, 2006): 1.

LOGIC OF ILLOGIC: YOU CAN'T MAKE ME EAT PIE

Brehm, Jack W. *A Theory of Psychological Reactance.* New York: Academic Press, 1966.

Dillard, James Pria, and Lijiang Shen. "On the Nature of Reactance and Its Role in Persuasive Health Communication." *Communication Monographs* 72, no. 2 (June 2005):144–168.

YOUR PERSONALIZED HOROSCOPE

Forer, Bertram R. "The Fallacy of Personal Validation: A Classroom Demonstration of Gullibility." *Journal of Abnormal and Social Psychology* 44 (January 1949):118–123.

E-PERSONALITY

Back, Mitja D., Stefan C. Schmukle, and Boris Egloff. "How Extraverted Is honey .bunny77@hotmail.de? Inferring Personality from E-mail Addresses." *Journal of Research in Personality* 42, no. 4 (August 2008):1116–1122.

FUZZY LOGIC

Zadeh, Lotfi A. "Is There a Need for Fuzzy Logic?" *Information Sciences* 178, no. 13 (July 2008):2751–2779.

ASCH CONFORMITY EXPERIMENTS

Asch, Solomon. "Opinions and Social Pressure." *Scientific American* 193, no. 5 (1955): 31–35.

WILD KINGDOM: GUPPY GAMES

Kelley, Jennifer L., et al. "Back to School: Can Antipredator Behaviour in Guppies Be Enhanced Through Social Learning?" *Animal Behaviour* 65, no. 4 (April 2003):655–662.

DEBUNKED: THE HAPPY HERD

Hamilton, W. D. "Geometry for the Selfish Herd." *Journal of Theoretical Biology* 31, no. 2 (May 1971):295–311.

GET OVER IT: THE END OF SHAME

Van Vliet, K. Jessica. "The Role of Attributions in the Process of Overcoming Shame: A Qualitative Analysis." *Psychology and Psychotherapy: Theory, Research and Practice* 82, no. 2 (June 2009):137–152.

THE ONE MUST OF HAPPINESS

Creagan, Edward. "On the Path to Finding Happiness." July 18, 2008. www.mayoclinic.com/health/happiness/MY00158.

"Achieving Fame, Wealth and Beauty Are Psychological Dead Ends, Study Says." ScienceDaily. May 19, 2009. www.sciencedaily.com/releases/2009/05/090514111402.htm.

TWINS AND SEX

"Emotional Intelligence 'Aids Sex.'" BBC News, online edition. May 12, 2009. news.bbc.co.uk/2/hi/health/8044571.stm.

GENETICS OF BEHAVIOR

Reiss, M. "The Genetics of Hand-Clasping—A Review and a Familial Study." *Annals of Human Biology* 26, no. 1 (Jan.–Feb. 1999):39–48.

Reiss, M. "Leg-Crossing: Incidence and Inheritance." *Neuropsychologia* 32, no. 6 (June 1994):747–750.

MEMORY I–III

Loftus, Elizabeth F., and John C. Palmer. "Reconstruction of Automobile Destruction: An Example of the Interaction Between Language and Memory." *Journal of Verbal*

Learning and Verbal Behavior 13 (1974):585–589.

Loftus, Elizabeth F., and G. Zanni. "Eyewitness Testimony: The Influence of the Wording of a Question." *Bulletin of the Psychonomic Society* 5 (1975): 86–88.

Loftus, Elizabeth F., D. Altman, and R. Geballe. "Effects of Questioning upon a Witness' Later Recollections." *Journal of Police Science and Administration* 3 (June 1975):162–165.

Okado, Y., and C. E. L. Stark. "Neural Activity During Encoding Predicts False Memories Created by Misinformation." *Learning and Memory* 12 (2005):3–11.

GENDER MEMORY SMACKDOWN

Loftus, Elizabeth F., Mahzarin B. Banaji, Jonathan W. Schooler, and Rachael A. Foster. "Who Remembers What? Gender Differences in Memory." *Michigan Quarterly Review* 26, no. 1 (Winter 1987):64–85.

LOGIC OF ILLOGIC: SO GOD-AWFULLY BORING

Festinger, Leon, and James W. Carlsmith. "Cognitive Consequences of Forced Compliance." *Journal of Abnormal and Social Psychology* 58 (1959):203–211.

POST-STEREOTYPE

Clark, Jason K., et al. "Discovering That the Shoe Fits: The Self-Validating Role of Stereotypes." *Psychological Science* 20, no. 7 (July 2009):846–852.

RACIAL BIAS IN STANDARDIZED TESTING?

Walton, Gregory, and Steven J. Spencer. "Latent Ability: Grades and Test Scores Systematically Underestimate the Intellectual Ability of Negatively Stereotyped Students."

Psychological Science 20, no. 9 (September 2009):1132–1139.

ALL WORK AND NO PLAY MAKES JACK'S BRAIN DULL

"Long Hours Lead to Dementia Risk." BBC News online. February 25, 2009. news.bbc .co.uk/2/hi/health/7909464.stm.

ACTION AND FREE WILL

Desmurget, Michel, et al. "Movement Intention After Parietal Cortex Stimulation in Humans." *Science* 324, no. 5928 (May 8, 2009):811–813.

PIECE OF MIND: CEREBELLUM

"Music as Food for the Brain." *Science* 282, no. 5393 (November 20, 1998): 1409.

Penhune, V. B., R. J. Zatorre, and A. C. Evans. "Cerebellar Contributions to Motor Timing: A PET Study of Auditory and Visual Rhythm Reproduction." *Journal of Cognitive Neuroscience* 10, no. 6 (November 1998): 752–765.

Gaab, Nadine, et al. "Functional Anatomy of Pitch Memory—An fMRI Study with Sparse Temporal Sampling." *NeuroImage* 19, no. 4 (August 2003):1417–1426.

DEBUNKED: DIAGNOSIS BATSHIT AND MISDIAGNOSIS: IMMUNITY

Rosenhan, David. "On Being Sane in Insane Places." *Science* 179, no. 4070 (January 19, 1973):250–8.

COFFEE AND CIGARETTES MAKE YOU SMARTER

Lorist, Monicque M., and Jan Snel. "Caffeine Effects on Perceptual and Motor Processes." *Electroencephalography and Clinical Neurophysiology* 102, no. 5 (May 1997):401–413.

Lorist, Monicque M., and Mattie Tops. "Caffeine, Fatigue, and Cognition." *Brain and Cognition* 53, no. 1 (October 2003):82–94.

Swan, Gary E., and Christina N. Lessov-Schlaggar. "The Effects of Tobacco Smoke and Nicotine on Cognition and the Brain." *Neuropsychology Review* 17, no. 3 (September 2007):259–273.

HOT OR NOT

Lee, Leonard, et al. "If I'm Not Hot, Are You Hot or Not? Physical-Attractiveness Evaluations and Dating Preferences as a Function of One's Own Attractiveness." *Psychological Science* 19, no. 7 (July 2008):669–677.

WILD KINGDOM: CHICKENS LIKE MODELS

"Poultry Prefer Pretty People." *Inpharma Weekly* 1668 (December 13, 2008):15.

IF YOU SAY SO: MEMORABLE LIES, FORGETTABLE TRUTHS

Allan, Kevin, and Fiona Gabbert. "I Still Think It Was a Banana: Memorable 'Lies' and Forgettable 'Truths.' " *Acta Psychologica* 127, no. 2 (February 2008):299–308.

WILD KINGDOM: HONOR AMONG THIEVES

"Vampire Bats Donate Blood." *Current Science* 76, no. 1 (September 7, 1990):9.

ABNORMAL PSYCH: CLIVE WEARING

Sacks, Oliver. "The Abyss." *New Yorker* 83, no. 28 (September 24, 2007):100–112.

GAME THEORY MAKE BRAIN BIG: EL FAROL BAR

Arthur, W. Brian. "Inductive Reasoning and Bounded Rationality." *American Economic Review* 84, no. 2 (May 1994):406–411.

THE DIET PARADOX: OFF-LIMITS IS OPEN SEASON

Soetens, Barbara, et al. "Resisting Temptation: Effects of Exposure to a Forbidden Food on Eating Behaviour." *Appetite* 51, no. 1 (July 2008):202–205.

THE FRENCH DIET

Wansink, Brian, Collin R. Payne, and Pierre Chandon. "Internal and External Cues of Meal Cessation: The French Paradox Redux?" *Obesity* 15, no. 12 (December, 2007):2920–2924.

ULTIMATE EVIL: NEUROIMAGING AS MARKET RESEARCH TOOL

Wilson, Mark, Jeannie Gaines, and Roland Hill. "Neuromarketing and Consumer Free Will." *Journal of Consumer Affairs* 42, no. 3 (Fall 2008): 389–410.

PIECE OF MIND: AMYGDALA

Guyer, Amanda E., et al. "A Developmental Examination of Amygdala Response to Facial Expressions." *Journal of Cognitive Neuroscience* 20, no. 9 (September 2008):1565–1582.

FUGHEDABOUDIT

Carey, Benedict. "Brain Researchers Open Door to Editing Memory." *New York Times* (April 5, 2009).

BAD MONKEY. NO CUCUMBER.

Range, Friederike, et al. "The Absence of Reward Induces Inequity Aversion in Dogs." *Proceedings of the National Academy of Sciences of the United States of America* 106, no. 1 (January 6, 2009):340–345.

WILD KINGDOM: HOOKNOSE JACK

Tanaka, Yumi, et al. "Breeding Games and Dimorphism in Male Salmon." *Animal Behaviour* 77, no. 6 (June 2009): 1409–1413.

Watters, Jason V. "Can the Alternative Male Tactics 'Fighter' and 'Sneaker' Be Considered 'Coercer' and 'Cooperator' in Coho Salmon?" *Animal Behaviour* 70, no. 5 (November 2005):1055–1062.

GAME THEORY MAKE BRAIN BIG: PIRATE PUZZLE

Stewart, Ian. "Mathematical Recreations: A Puzzle for Pirates." *Scientific American* 280, no. 5 (May 1999):98.

BLINDSIGHT

Carey, Benedict. "Blind, Yet Seeing: The Brain's Subconscious Visual Sense." *New York Times* (December 23, 2008): 5.

PIECE OF MIND: OCCIPITAL LOBE

Ueno, Aya, et al. "Reactivation of Medial Temporal Lobe and

Occipital Lobe During the Retrieval of Color Information: A Positron Emission Tomography Study." *NeuroImage* 34, no. 3 (February 2007): 1292–1298.

INTUITION TRUMPS REASON: THE IOWA GAMBLING TASK

Bechara, A., et al. "Insensitivity to Future Consequences Following Damage to Human Prefrontal Cortex." *Cognition* 50 (1994):7–15.

Evans, Cathryn E. Y., Karen Kemish, and Oliver H. Turnbull. "Paradoxical Effects of Education on the Iowa Gambling Task." *Brain and Cognition* 54, no. 3 (April 2004):240–244.

Turnbull, Oliver H., et al. "Emotion-Based Learning and Central Executive Resources: An Investigation of Intuition and the Iowa Gambling Task." *Brain and Cognition* 57, no. 3 (April 2005):244–247.

Vadhan, Nehal P., et al. "Decision-Making in Long-Term Cocaine Users: Effects of a Cash Monetary Contingency on Gambling Task Performance." *Drug and Alcohol Dependence* 102, no. 1–3 (June 2009): 95–101.

Gupta, Rupa, et al. "Declarative Memory Is Critical for Sustained Advantageous Complex Decision-Making." *Neuropsychologia* 47, no. 7 (June 2009):1686–1693.

THE TRANSFORMATIVE POWER OF THE UNEXPECTED

Zaghloul, Kareem A., et al. "Human Substantia Nigra Neurons Encode Unexpected Financial Rewards." *Science* 323, no. 5920 (March 13, 2009):1496–1499.

HANDWRITING ANALYSIS

Berwick, Donald M., and David E. Winickoff. "The Truth

About Doctors' Handwriting: A Prospective Study." *BMJ: British Medical Journal* 313, no. 7072 (December 21, 1996): 1657–1658.

BRAIN SWEAT

Gallup, Andrew C., Michael L. Miller, and Anne B. Clark. "Yawning and Thermoregulation in Budgerigars, *Melopsittacus undulatus.*" *Animal Behaviour* 77, no. 1 (January 2009):109–113.

YOUR BRAIN ON SPACE

Gabrion, Jaqueline. "Choroidal Regulation: Understanding Fluid Shifts in the Brain." weboflife.nasa.gov/currentResearch/currentResearchFlight/sts107Choroidal.htm.

PIECE OF MIND: PARIETAL LOBE

Phan, M. L., et al. "Auditory and Visual Spatial Localization Deficits Following Bilateral Parietal Lobe Lesions in a Patient with Balint's Syndrome." *Journal of Cognitive Neuroscience* 12, no. 4 (July 2000):583–600.

Koscik, Tim, et al. "Sex Differences in Parietal Lobe Morphology: Relationship to Mental Rotation Performance." *Brain and Cognition* 69, no. 3 (April 2009):451–459.

AUTISM AND LEGOS

Wheelwright, Sally, and Simon Baron-Cohen. "The Link Between Autism and Skills Such as Engineering, Maths, Physics, and Computing: A Reply to Jarrold and Reuth." *Autism: The International Journal of Research and Practice* 5, no. 2 (June 2001):223–227.

MALES' RAT-BRAINED NAVIGATION

Grön, Georg, et al. "Brain Activation During Human Navigation: Gender-Different Neural Networks as Substrate of Performance." *Nature Neuroscience* 3, no. 4 (April 2000):404–408.

THE KNOWLEDGE

Maguire, Eleanor A., et al. "Navigation-Related Structural Change in the Hippocampi of Taxi Drivers." *Proceedings of the National Academy of Sciences of the United States of America* 97, no. 8 (April 11, 2000): 4398–4403.

THE BRAINWORKS OF RELIGIOUS CONVICTION AND ECSTASY

Inzlicht, Michael, et al. "Neural Markers of Religious Conviction." *Psychological*

Science 20, no. 3 (March 2009): 385–392.

Johnstone, Brick, and Bret A. Glass. "Support for a Neuropsychological Model of Spirituality in Persons with Traumatic Brain Injury." *Zygon: Journal of Religion & Science* 43, no. 4 (December 2008):861–874.

THE MEDITATIVE MIND

Wheeler, Mark. "How to Build a Bigger Brain: Meditation May Increase Gray Matter." May 12, 2009. newsroom.ucla .edu/portal/ucla/how-to-build-a -bigger-brain-91273.aspx.

I CHOOSE MY CHOICE

Sharot, Tali, Benedetto De Martino, and Raymond J. Dolan. "How Choice Reveals and Shapes Expected Hedonic Outcome." *Journal of Neuroscience* 29, no. 12 (March 25, 2009): 3760–3765.

FEAR-THEN-RELIEF PRISONER COMPLIANCE

Dolinski, Dariusz, and Richard Nawrat. "'Fear-Then-Relief' Procedure for Producing Compliance: Beware When the Danger Is Over." *Journal of Experimental Social Psychology* 34, no. 1 (January 1998):27–50.

PIECE OF MIND: MEDULLA OBLONGATA

Eippert, Falk, et al. "Activation of the Opioidergic Descending Pain Control System Underlies Placebo Analgesia." *Neuron* 63, no. 4 (August 27, 2009): 533–543.

PLACEBOS ARE GETTING STRONGER

Silberman, Steve. "Placebos Are Getting More Effective. Drugmakers Are Desperate to Know Why." *Wired* (August 24, 2009): wired.com/medtech/drugs/magazine/17-09/ff_placebo_effect?currentPage=all.

MEERKATS, MACAQUES, MEN, AND THE HEALING EFFECTS OF FORGIVENESS

Kutsukake, Nobuyuki, and Tim H. Clutton-Brock. "Do Meerkats Engage in Conflict Management Following Aggression? Reconciliation, Submission and Avoidance." *Animal Behaviour* 75, no. 4 (April 2008): 1441–1453.

Pereira, Michael E., Jennifer L. Schill, and Eric P. Charles. "Reconciliation in Captive Guyanese Squirrel Monkeys (*Saimiri sciureus*)." *American Journal of Primatology* 50, no. 2 (February 2000):159–167.

Lawler-Row, Kathleen A., et al. "Forgiveness, Physiological Reactivity and Health: The Role of Anger." *International Journal of Psychophysiology* 68, no. 1 (April 2008):51–58.

WILD KINGDOM: REVENGE!

McCullough, Michael. *Beyond Revenge: The Evolution of the Forgiveness Instinct.* San Francisco, Cal.: Jossey-Bass, 2008.

NEUROETHICS

Greely, Henry. "Prediction, Litigation, Privacy, and Property: Some Possible Legal and Social Implications of Advances in Neuroscience." Remarks for the Regan lecture. scu.edu/ethics/publications/submitted/greely/neuroscience_ethics_law.html.

Brunner, H. G., et al. "Abnormal Behavior Associated with a Point Mutation in the Structural Gene for Monoamine Oxidase A." *Science* 262, no. 5133 (October 22, 1993):578–580.

Denno, Deborah W. "Human Biology and Criminal Responsibility: Free Will or Free Ride?" *University of Pennsylvania Law Review* 137, no. 2 (December 1988):615–671.

FACEBOOK SEXUALITY PREDICTION

Johnson, Carolyn. "Project 'Gaydar.'" *Boston Globe,* online edition (September 20, 2009): www.tinyurl.com-projectgaydar.

I WOULD NEVER

Carey, Benedict. "Stumbling Blocks on the Path of Righteousness." *New York Times* (May 5, 2009):D5.

WILL AND GRACE

Greene, Joshua D., and Joseph M. Paxton. "Patterns of Neural Activity Associated with Honest and Dishonest Moral Decisions." *Proceedings of the National Academy of Sciences of the United States of America* 109, no. 3 (July 28, 2009):12506–12511.

MEMORIZATION 101

Carrier, L. Mark, and Harold Pashler. "Attentional Limits in Memory Retrieval." *Journal of Experimental Psychology: Learning, Memory, and Cognition* 21, no. 5 (September 1995):1339–1348.

DOES SUBLIMINAL ADVERTISING WORK?

Karremans, Johan C., Wolfgang Stroebe, and Jasper Claus. "Beyond Vicary's Fantasies: The Impact of Subliminal Priming and Brand Choice." *Journal of Experimental Social Psychology* 42, no. 6 (November 2006): 792–798.

Byrne, Donn. "The Effect of a Subliminal Food Stimulus on Verbal Responses." *Journal of Applied Psychology* 43, no. 4 (1959):249–251.

Bermeitinger, Christina, et al. "The Hidden Persuaders Break into the Tired Brain." *Journal of Experimental Social Psychology* 45, no. 2 (February 2009): 320–326.

LOGIC OF ILLOGIC: K WORDS

Tversky, Amos, and Daniel Kahneman. "Judgment Under Uncertainty: Heuristics and Biases." *Science,* 185 no. 4157 (September 27, 1974): 1124–1131.

GENIUS TESTER #10: THE PSYCHOLOGY OF GETTING SUCKERED

Tierney, John. "The Psychology of Getting Suckered." tierneylab .blogs.nytimes.com/2008/04/ 10/the-psychology-of-getting -suckered/.

ANIMAL KINGDOM: PIGEON AFICIONADO

Watanabe, Shigeru, Junko Sakamoto, and Masumi Wakita. "Pigeons' Discrimination of Paintings by Monet and Picasso." *Journal of the Experimental Analysis of Behavior* 63, no. 2 (March 1995):165–174.

NEURAL DARWINISM

Edelman, Gerald. *Neural Darwinism: The Theory of Neuronal Group Selection*. New York: Basic Books, 1987.

STRETCHING PHANTOM LIMB CRAMPS

Colapinto, John. "Brain Games." *New Yorker* 85, no. 13 (May 11, 2009):76–87.

WILD KINGDOM: ANALYTIC ANTS

Edwards, Susan C., and Stephen C. Pratt. "Rationality in Collective Decision-Making by Ant Colonies." *Proceedings of the Royal Society B: Biological Sciences* 276, no. 1673 (October 22, 2009):3655–3661.

LOGIC OF ILLOGIC: FRUIT BAG

Ellsberg, Daniel. "Risk, Ambiguity, and the Savage Axioms." *Quarterly Journal of Economics* 75, no. 4 (November 1961):643–699.

ABNORMAL PSYCH: PHINEAS GAGE

"The Incredible Case of Phineas Gage." December 4, 2006. neurophilosophy.wordpress .com/2006/12/04/the-incredible -case-of-phineas-gage/.

IS LAUGHTER THE BEST MEDICINE?

Krupa, Donna. "Laughter Remains Good Medicine: New Study Reports on the Mind-Emotion-Disease Model." www .eurekalert.org/pub_releases/ 2009–04/aps-lrg041509.php.

THE IMPACT OF TRAGEDY

Vedantam, Shankar. "In the Face of Tragedy: Moral Reasoning Along 'Whodunit' Lines." *Washington Post* (December 8, 2008): A14.

BAD POETRY AIDS RECOVERY

Alleyne, Richard. "AAAS: Writing Poems Helps Brain Cope with Emotional Turmoil, Say Scientists." www.telegraph .co.uk/culture/culturenews/ 4630043/AAAS-Writing -poems-helps-brain-cope-with -emotional-turmoil-say -scientists.html.

HORROR FILM PTSD

Holmes, Emily A., and Corin Bourne. "Inducing and Modulating Intrusive Emotional Memories: A Review of the Trauma Film Paradigm." *Acta*

Psychologica 127, no. 3 (March 2008):553–566.

FRUIT VS. VEGGIE PERSONALITY SMACKDOWN

"Vegetable Lovers Should Be Viewed as Different from Fruit Aficionados." ScienceDaily (November 16, 2004): www.sciencedaily.com/ releases/2004/11/041115002000 .htm.

DEFLECTING INCOMING BLOOPERS

Mazaheri, Ali, et al. "Prestimulus Alpha and Mu Activity Predicts Failure to Inhibit Motor Responses." *Human Brain Mapping* 30, no. 6 (April 2009):1791–1800.

THE BURDEN OF CONVENTIONAL THINKING

Gladwell, Malcolm. "How David Beats Goliath." *New Yorker* 85, no. 13 (May 11, 2009):40–49.

TIME TRAVEL: SCIENCE, NOT SCIENCE FICTION

Boyer, Pascal. "Evolutionary Economics of Mental Time Travel?" *Trends in Cognitive Sciences* 12, no. 6 (June 2008):219–224.

THE AGE OF TIME TRAVEL

Busby, Janie, and Thomas Suddendorf. "Recalling Yesterday and Predicting Tomorrow." *Cognitive Development* 20, no. 3 (July 2005):362–372.

ACTIVE FORGETTING: THE MENTAL BOXES OF SUPPRESSION AND REPRESSION

Wegner, Daniel, and Sophia Zanakos. "Chronic Thought Suppression." *Journal of Personality* 62 (December 1994):615–640.

IGNORING IS EXHAUSTING

Tierney, John. "Ear Plugs to Lasers: The Science of Concentration." *New York Times* (May 5, 2009):D2.

Anderson, Michael C., and Benjamin J. Levy. "Suppressing Unwanted Memories." *Current Directions in Psychological Science* 18, no. 4 (August 2009):189–194.

EXERCISE MAKES YOU SMART

Lou, Shu-jie, et al. "Hippocampal Neurogenesis and Gene Expression Depend on Exercise Intensity in Juvenile Rats." *Brain Research* 1210 (May 19, 2008):48–55.

Tomporowski, Phillip D. "Effects of Acute Bouts of Exercise on Cognition." *Acta Psychologica* 112, no. 3 (March 2003):297–324.

Cotman, Carl W., and Nicole C. Berchtold. "Exercise: A Behavioral Intervention to Enhance Brain Health and Plasticity." *Trends in Neurosciences* 25, no. 6 (June 1, 2002):295–301.

DO CROSSWORDS KEEP THE BRAIN YOUNG?

McNab, Fiona, et al. "Changes in Cortical Dopamine D1 Receptor Binding Associated with Cognitive Training." *Science* 323, no. 5915 (February 6, 2009):800–802.

I SHOP, THEREFORE I AM

Zhao, Shanyang, Sherri Grasmuck, and Jason Martin. "Identity Construction on Facebook: Digital Empowerment in Anchored Relationships." *Computers in Human Behavior* 24, no. 5 (September 2008):1816–1836.

"We Are What We Buy, Says Sociologist." *Guardian UK,* online edition (December 19, 2002): www.guardian .co.uk/education/2002/dec/19/ highereducation.uk2.

GENIUS TESTER #11: THE MONTY HALL PROBLEM

Brown, Thad A., and Donald Granberg. "The Monty Hall Dilemma." *Personality and Social Psychology Bulletin* 21, no. 7 (1995):711–723.

BIOLOGICAL BASIS OF ROSE-COLORED GLASSES

St. Jacques, Peggy L., Florin Dolcos, and Roberto Cabeza. "Effects of Aging on Functional Connectivity of the Amygdala for Subsequent Memory of Negative Pictures: A Network Analysis of Functional Magnetic Resonance Imaging Data." *Psychological Science* 20, no. 1 (January 2009):74–84.

THE FUNCTION OF DAYDREAMS

"Brain's Problem-solving Function at Work When We Daydream." *ScienceDaily* (May 12, 2009): sciencedaily.com/releases/2009/05/090511180702.htm.

THE COLLECTIVE UNCONSCIOUS

Jung, Carl. *The Collected Works of C.G. Jung.* Volume

9. Princeton, NJ: Princeton University Press, 1969.

Keyes, Ken. *The Hundredth Monkey.* St. Mary, Ky.: Vision Books, 1981.

BRAINWASHING THE EASY WAY

Zimbardo, Phillip. "What Messages Are Behind Today's Cults?" *APA Monitor* 14 (May 1997): www.csj.org/studyindex/studycult/study_zimbar.htm.

MODERN DEHUMANIZATION

Costigan, Genevieve. "The Psychology of Dehumanization." *University of Melbourne Voice* 5, no. 6 (September–October 2009): voice.unimelb.edu.au/news/5894/.

WILD KINGDOM: AMOROUS OSTRICHES

Bubier, N. E., et al. "Courtship Behaviour of Ostriches (*Struthio camelus*) Towards Humans under Farming Conditions in Britain." *British Poultry Science* 39, no. 4 (August 1998): 477–481.

FOUR STEPS TO PERSUASION

Jones, Dan, and Alison Motluck. "How to Get Exactly What You Want." *New Scientist* 198, no. 2655 (May 10, 2008):32–37.

Goldstein, Noah J., Steve J. Martin, and Robert B. Cialdini. *Yes! 50 Scientifically Proven Ways to Be Persuasive.* New York: Free Press, 2008.

LOGIC OF ILLOGIC: THE END IS NEAR

Festinger, Leon, Henry W. Riecken, and Stanley Schachter. *When Prophecy Fails: A Social and Psychological Study of a Modern Group That Predicted the Destruction of the World.* Minneapolis: University of Minnesota Press, 1956.

WHIFFLE BALL CROTCH SHOT

Hsu, Jeremy. "Brain Struggles with Social Compassion." April 17, 2009: www.livescience.com/culture/090417-gentle-emotions.html.

MUSIC, COMMERCE, AND MURDER

Levitin, Daniel J. "Do You Hear What I Hear?" *Wall Street Journal* 252, no. 140 (December 13, 2008):W1–W2.

WILD KINGDOM: MOSQUITOES' DOUBLE DUTCH

Dixon, Bernard. "Cheese, Toes, and Mosquitoes." *BMJ: British Medical Journal* 312, no. 7038 (April 27, 1996):1105.

UN-APOLOGY APOLOGY

Pope, Kenneth S., and Melba J. T. Vasquez. *Ethics in Psychotherapy and Counseling: A Practical Guide.* San Francisco, Cal.: Jossey-Bass/John Wiley & Sons, 2007.

WILD KINGDOM: IMPOLITE HERRING

Wilson, Ben, Robert S. Batty, and Lawrence M. Dill. "Pacific and Atlantic Herring Produce Burst Pulse Sounds." *Proceedings of the Royal Society B: Biological Sciences* 271 (February 2, 2004):S95–S97.

ANYTHING YOU CAN DO, I CAN DO BADDER

Keysar, Boaz, et al. "Reciprocity Is Not Give and Take: Asymmetric Reciprocity to Positive and Negative Acts." *Psychological Science* 19, no. 12 (December 2008):1280–1286.

HOW TO *REALLY* SPOT A LIAR

Carey, Benedict. "Judging Honesty by Words, Not Fidgets." *New York Times* (May 12, 2009):D1.

COUNTER-PRODUCTIVE COERCION

O'Mara, Shane. "Torturing the Brain: On the Folk Psychology and Folk Neurobiology Motivating 'Enhanced and Coercive Interrogation Techniques.' " *Trends in Cognitive*

Science 13, no. 12 (December 2009):497–500.

SEQUENTIAL BLIND LINEUP

Emily, Jennifer. "Dallas Police Drop Study, Plan Photo Lineup Changes." *Dallas Morning News* (January 16, 2009): www .dallasnews.com/sharedcontent/ dws/news/localnews/stories/ 011609dnmetsequentialblind .4311ff6.html.

RED BEATS BLUE AT THE OLYMPICS

Dambeck, Holger. "The Annals of Sports Psychology: Winners Wear Red." August 8, 2008: www.spiegel.de/international/ zeitgeist/0,1518,570918,00.html.

OFFICE DECOR: BEYOND FENG SHUI

Mehta, Ravi, and Rui Zhu. "Blue or Red? Exploring the Effect of Color on Cognitive Task Performance." *Science* 323 (February 27, 2009):1226–1229.

NEUROLOGICAL SUPPORT FOR THE USE OF SHOE SMELL IN CONTROLLING EPILEPTIC SEIZURE

Jaseja, Harinder. "Scientific Basis Behind Traditional Practice of Application of 'shoe-smell' in Controlling Epileptic Seizures in the Eastern Countries." *Clinical Neurology and Neurosurgery* 110, no. 6 (June 2008):535–538.

SEIZURE AND THE GENDER SWITCH

Kasper, B. S., et al. "Ictal Delusion of Sexual Transformation." *Epilepsy & Behavior* 16, no. 2 (October 2009):356–359. 10.1016/j.yebeh .2009.07.024.

ACKNOWLEDGMENTS

First, thanks to all the neuroscientists, psychologists, economists, computer scientists, engineers, etc. whose fascinating work makes a book like this tremendously fun to write. And thanks, too, to the listservs, databases, and science-minded publications that make their work accessible, with special shout-outs to the psychologist Ken Pope, *New York Times* writers Benedict Carey and John Tierney, the WNYC program *Radiolab,* the database ScienceDirect and the blog ScientificBlogging.com (where I write), all of which I mined at times for ideas. Thanks to Kristi and Mom for giving me psychology heads-ups and to Dad for providing the economics and game-theory counterpoint. And I'd like to recognize all the folks at Three Rivers who helped me shape and produce *Brain Candy*—my editor, Julian Pavia, for forcing me to get to the point; Dyana Messina, for helping people find the book; Philip Patrick, whose benediction I've felt from afar; book designer Maria Elias, who must've been horrified when this art-heavy layout nightmare landed on her desk; and production editor Rachelle Mandik, for her help beating aforementioned layout into shape. And thanks to Jen, my agent, who continues to leap buildings in a single bound, even without the phone booth of a reasonable economy to launch from.

TUNE IN.
TURN ON.
GEEK OUT.

Finally, here's the book no self-respecting geek can live without—a guide jam-packed with 314.1516 short entries both useful and fun. Science, pop-culture trivia, paper airplanes, and pure geekish nostalgia coexist in this book as happily as they do in their natural habitat of the geek brain.

• build a laser beam • clone your pet • find the world's best corn mazes • have sex in Second Life • kick ass with sweet martial-arts moves • pimp your cubicle • visit Beaver Lick, Kentucky • write your name in Elvish

Join us or die, you will.
Begun, the Geek Wars have.

The Geeks' Guide
to World Domination
Be Afraid, Beautiful People

$13.95 paperback (Canada: $15.95)

978-0-307-45034-0

Available from Three Rivers Press wherever books are sold